To Adrienne,

[signature] Brandon Wichman

Breaking Chains

Brandon Wichman

My Family

God has blessed me with an awesome fiancée, Sarah. We will be getting married this year!

With my parents and brother on his graduation day.

My Ministry

Check out other books I have written at:

www.thebrandonwichmancompany.com

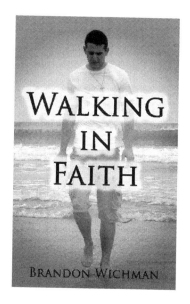

Thank You!

    While my name may be on the cover of this book as the author, I want all of you readers to know that there are many amazing people in my life who contributed their time and effort to make this book what it is today.

    First, and most importantly, I want to thank God for the opportunity He has given me to pursue ministry. I also want to thank my fiancée, Sarah, for encouraging me to keep writing even when finding time was challenging. She also did an excellent job of editing this book which I will always be thankful for.

    I also want to thank all of my family and friends who played a role in making this book what it is today. You are all amazing blessings, and I love every one of you!

    Lastly, I would like to thank all of the readers who have followed my work throughout the last couple of years. Much of the encouragement to keep writing has come from you. Thank you for all of the stories you have shared and the joy you have brought to my life. I really appreciate it and hope that this book will be a blessing to you as much as the last ones were!

Contents

Introduction

T ODAY IS THE start of a new journey. A journey with a purpose. I don't know what has led you to pick up this book, but I am extremely glad you did. When you first saw this book, you may have wondered what it is really about. What is the whole meaning behind *Breaking Chains*? What are these chains? Answering questions like these will set the stage for how to interpret and understand these devotions, so please flip back to this page if you ever forget what chains are. Here is the key definition for the topic of this book:

Chains: *Elements of this sinful world that pull us away from God.*

With that definition in mind, my hope is that you will grow to see the beauty in this journey as you progress from chapter to chapter. We are surrounded and consumed by sins and struggles. There is no way to completely block out or do away with the elements of life that lead us to sin. We simply can't do it. Sin is a part of the world we live in and that will never change. But we must never forget the rock-solid truth that gives hope to all who take hold of it. The truth is that the amazing hope of Heaven is ours because of the life, death, and resurrection of Jesus Christ. He paid the price so we could be freed from this world that does everything it can to chain us down. Satan will use anything and everything he can to trip us up. He wants us to take on our struggles within and block out any source of relief. When it comes to breaking the chains of this life, there is only one way that will ever happen. We need to call on Jesus. We need Him! The devil will use all 11 chains in this book with the hope that we will try to battle him one-on-one. He knows you have faith, and he knows you will fight. This book is not simply about battling with your struggles. It is about *how* you approach them.

The reality of life on Earth is that we all have a cross to bear. We all have something in our lives that serves as a distraction in our relationships with God. You may struggle with drinking or drugs. Maybe you are addicted to pornography or struggle with some other addiction. Whatever your struggle is, I want you to know that this devotional book is designed for you. The reason I can say that is because the topics within each chapter run deeper than one struggle or shortfall. The chains in this book focus on the most common struggles that God's people face. That being said, I want you to know all of the chains in this book are not necessarily sins. For example, living a complex lifestyle, in and of itself, is not a sin. There is nothing wrong with having a booming career while trying to balance family life along with other interests. However, the devil does like to use a busy lifestyle to convince us that we don't have time for God. Satan wants us to believe that we are justified for missing church last week because we had a sporting event to go to. You may be able to relate to having a complex lifestyle, which is exactly why this topic is one of the chains in this book. The devil will use something as simple as busyness to pull us away from God, which sadly works far too often.

As you go through each chapter, you will engage with a topic that may or may not be close to your heart. For example, you may struggle with balancing a complex lifestyle far more often than pride or anger. We all have different sets of struggles that we face. However, my encouragement for you is to read every chapter as if your struggle with the chain is personal. I learned a lot about myself in the process of writing this book. As you go from chapter to chapter, the chances are pretty good that you will come across a chain that is more present in your life than you thought. For example, I never really considered myself the type to struggle with balancing a complex lifestyle. After researching this topic, writing on it, and then reading what I wrote at a later time, I realized this was a chain in my life that was not getting much, if any, attention. Discovering flaws within yourself may sound dark and depressing, but let me tell you this: when you dig deep and face the chains that are pulling you away from God, it is way easier to go to Him in prayer and ask for help. No battle with sin can be fought alone, but every struggle can be overcome with the help of Jesus. My hope and prayer for this journey is that your connection with God grows stronger every step of the way.

Spiritual Heart Disease

Day 1

Give Praise for the Day

24 This is the day that the Lord has made;
let us rejoice and be glad in it.

-Psalm 118:24, ESV

IT IS MONDAY morning. You have to get up early for work. It is raining. Your throat is sore and you didn't sleep well last night. What is your mental approach to a day like this? For me, these drowsy and dreary mornings are not normally approached with a go-getter attitude. I often try to pull it together, but too often my efforts fail. Those failed efforts and poor attitudes are something I call *Spiritual Heart Disease*.

As we face struggles that cause strain in our relationships with God, it is critically important to focus our hearts on rejoicing in the Lord. We live in a sinful world that often looks at the bad much more than the good. As Christians, we can see and know that every day is a blessing. God has a plan for every one of us, and every day has a purpose. It can be extremely easy to question God and ask why He allows us to have tough days that involve seemingly endless difficult situations. However, we know through faith that our Father in Heaven loves us and works all things out for our good.

As you dive forward into this chapter of devotions about seeking healing to Spiritual Heart Disease, I want to encourage you to give thanks for all of the blessings God provides you with every day. And I'm not just talking about the blessings you enjoy or the ones that are pleasant. Give thanks to God for the little trials He uses to build you up and make you stronger. Never forget that today is a day that the Lord has made! Our loving God planned out each day of our lives long before we even existed. He knows our needs, and He wants us to grow closer to Him.

So...you may have wondered at some point throughout this

devotion why I decided to start with a topic like spiritual heart disease. While it may seem like a downer, I promise there is a good reason. Oftentimes, our attitudes are the very aspect of our beings that drag us down in our lives of faith. A heart that doesn't adhere to and embrace the love of God will cease and crumble just like our physical heart does when we don't take care of it. When it comes to battling the strains of this life, having a heart that not just understands, but truly believes that God is there for us and loves us is key.

As a follower of Christ, I know that my thought process on those tough mornings should go something like this:

> *"I have the privilege of getting up early for the job I am blessed with. I am a little tired, but it's not a problem. I'll make a point of going to bed early tonight. It is raining, but no worries! I have an umbrella. My throat is a little scratchy, but it's no big deal. I have medicine that should clear things up in a few days."*

This is the day the Lord has made! Rejoice and be glad in it!

Prayer

Dear Father in Heaven, please help us to live every day in a manner that embraces Your love. All too often we look at the negative aspects of our day and ignore all the positives. Every day is a gift from You, and we ask you to help us treat our days as the tremendous blessings they are. In the name of Jesus we pray. Amen.

Personal Reflection

Think of one individual blessing to thank God for today. Write it down and reflect on that blessing throughout the week.

Day 2

Medication for the Soul

²² A cheerful heart is good medicine,
but a crushed spirit dries up the bones.

-Proverbs 17:22

L IFE IS FULL of trials that challenge us and oftentimes puncture our spirits. For many people, health problems rattle them right to their core. When a heart attack, cancer, or diabetes show up without warning, keeping one's composure can be very difficult. There are diseases in this world that no pill or treatment can cure, but does that mean all hope is lost?

My grandfather is one of the most prominent role models in my life. He has taught me a lot about life in countless ways. Among all of the lessons and values he has impressed upon me, nothing compares to the importance this man places on a positive attitude.

Grandpa has faced many health issues over the course of his eighty plus years on this earth. He has had seven heart attacks and many other health difficulties. Death has been at this man's door many times, and you have to wonder what is keeping him going. One of the obvious answers to this question is that God is not done with him yet, but is there another secret to life that my grandfather holds?

Joy. If one word could define my grandpa, Vern Wichman, it is joy. Every day has a purpose and every day is an opportunity to do something. Grandpa has been through the ringer of life by the standards of most people. The human body can only take so much wear and tear before it gives out. I often look at my grandpa and wonder how in the world he is still going. If you would ask him how or why he is still living today, he would say it's because of his attitude. Even doctors and nurses over his 30 plus year battle with heart disease have said that his positive attitude has kept him going. There were many times he could have given up and let go of his will to live. I have seen Grandpa so weak that it's a wonder he had a will to live, but his cheerful heart kept him going. I can't give you a better testimony of why attitude truly matters than this.

A strong faith in God gives mankind a source of blessing that provides what we need to survive in this world. A heart that is downcast and hopeless not only dries up our physical bones, but hardens our hearts as well. As we go through each day, there are countless blessings to be thankful for and to cherish. We will all face challenges that will try to crush our spirits, but my encouragement for you today is to look at my grandfather as an example of what a cheerful heart can bring. Grandpa is one of the happiest people I know, and there is no doubt in my mind that his faith-driven attitude is the source of his joy.

Prayer

Dear Lord, thank You for another day of Your amazing grace. This life is full of struggles and hardships, and we often let those things crush our spirits. We ask that You guide us to be cheerful and to embrace the amazing gift of unending love that is found in Jesus. It is in His name we pray. Amen.

Personal Reflection

Think of a time when your spirits were crushed and you felt hopeless. What had you down, and how would the attitude of this proverb impact similar situations in the future?

Day 3

God's Workmanship

*14 I praise you because I am fearfully and wonderfully
made; your works are wonderful, I know that full well.*
-Psalm 139:14

D O YOU EVER stare in the mirror and think you look like an absolute
disaster? Your hair is a mess to a degree where it looks
unfixable. You have so much acne that it looks like a pimple bomb
blew up all over your face. Maybe you struggle with your weight or
are lacking desired gifts and talents. Perceived flaws or shortcomings
generally cause us to wish we could be something more. Something
better.

It would be nearly impossible to find someone who is 100%
satisfied with the body God has given them. I look at myself in the
mirror every day and often see the flaws before anything else. I fixate
on the pimples or moles on my face instead of thanking God for the
body He has given me. The odds are very good that you have done the
same thing, and now it is time for us to both face a rather serious
question: are we better at praising God for what we have, or asking
Him for what we don't have?

As we dig into this verse from Psalm 139, I really want to encourage
you to reflect on these powerful words. We are *fearfully* and
wonderfully made by a God who loves us more than we can
comprehend! We have so much to be thankful for, but are we really
thankful?

It can be difficult to thank and praise God when discontent burdens
our hearts, but there are some truly amazing realities we should never
forget. Regardless of your gifts and talents, remember that God made
you the way you are for a reason. God doesn't make garbage. The
work of the Holy Spirit within every believer's heart (including yours)

is amazing. We may not always get to see the true beauty behind God's work within us, but we can always be confident through faith that His blessings are present in our lives.

As you work through the rest of this chapter, I want to encourage you to embrace an attitude that reflects the work of our loving God. You can always be assured that you are abundantly blessed because God's spirit lives in you. No matter how many flaws we see in the mirror, there is no doubt we all have more blessings than we could ever truly ask for.

Prayer

Dear Creator of all, thank You for the body, soul, mind, and abilities You have given me. All too often I look at myself and wish I was different. I desire more and fail to see the wonders of Your creation. I ask that You guide my heart to see how I am special because of Your work within me. In the name of Your Son I pray. Amen.

Personal Reflection

Reflect on one gift or ability that God has blessed you with. Think of how this attribute of your being has been a blessing to you. What does this feature allow you to do? How can you praise God with this gift? And lastly, thank God for this talent that He has graciously given you!

Day 4

Embrace His Plan

11 For I know the plans I have for you," declares the Lord, "plans to prosper you and not to harm you, plans to give you hope and a future.

-Jeremiah 29:11

T HE VERSE ABOVE is my favorite verse in the entire Bible. I have needed these words as a reminder countless times in recent years. I am a planner who likes to know what is ahead and how I can get there, but God's Word reveals a different reality about the future. Our Father in Heaven is the One who has the reins and is steering our lives where they need to go. Trusting God's plan has been very difficult for me at times, but it has definitely been a tremendous blessing.

My college years have taught me more about how God works than any other period of my life so far. The Lord has used several aspects of my life to teach me why His plan is best. For example, I can remember going into college thinking that I would be studying psychology for six years. My plan was to get my master's degree and to be a counselor. All in all, that sounds like a good plan, but it was through these plans being broken that I gained a better understanding of why God's plan is better. It only took me a few weeks of college to realize that the field of psychology was not for me. I switched schools twice before I found my final landing place at Lakeland University. I have met great people, am the happiest I have been in my college career, and am thriving in an environment that fits me very well. God knew what He was doing when He threw me some curves balls, and I have come to trust Him more because of the journey He laid out for me.

My college experience is one that I would consider to be a much easier journey than the one found within the context of these verses.

While the situation concerning my college career seemed pretty intense and stressful at the time, it does not even compare to the situation Jeremiah was facing in this passage. He was writing to people who were carried out of Jerusalem by King Nebuchadnezzar to face exile in Babylon. In other words, these people were forced away from their homes and were now slaves. In this letter, God inspired Jeremiah with words to assure these exiles that God had a plan for them. In extreme situations, it can be really hard to see how God is working things out for our good, but that doesn't change reality. God is always there for us. We all have hope because the Creator of the universe has a perfect plan for every one of us. A heart that trusts God is key to thriving in our lives of faith. The journey to breaking chains is one that demands trust in God's will for our lives. Our hearts may all be stained with spiritual heart disease, but we can be assured through faith that we have direction. God is with us and will guide us where He wants us to go. Trusting our Father in Heaven is not always easy, but we can be confident He will lead us where we need to go.

Prayer
Dear God, please guide my heart to trust Your plan in every situation. Amen.

Personal Reflection
Identify one plan you have made for your life that didn't work out the way you wanted it to. How did God's plan take precedence over your plan? Were you able to see the blessing in God's plan?

Day 5

Effective Satan Repellent

⁷ Submit yourselves, then, to God. Resist the devil, and he will flee from you.

-James 4:7

TODAY WE ARE going to address one of the dirty words of 21ˢᵗ century America. That's right, the "s" word. *Submit.* There are not many corners within our society that take too kindly to this word. It is considered to be oppressive and offensive if used in the context of male/female relationships or really in any context at all. While the world may oppose this word and give it a bad rap, we need to get real about what this word means to us as Christians. A heart that opposes submission in our relationships with God is one that denies who is really in control. Yesterday's devotion was all about putting our trust in God's plan. Now, we are going to take a step even deeper into this chain of a spiritual heart disease by evaluating a key way we can stay close to God. Full submission. All in with the cards on the table. Completely vulnerable. This may sound really scary, but as one digs into what submission to God really is, it becomes evident that the blessings which come with submission are abundant.

To get a better understanding of what I mean by submit, let's take a look at what the word really means. Our world often takes this word in a context of a "forceful" or "destructive" or "demanding" attitude. If you read the book of James, you will see that this book is all about putting faith in motion. Submission within the context of this verse is not God forcing us under His wing, but rather is an embrace to willingly follow the Lord's will in everything. Completely yielding ourselves to God can be really hard, but never forget the protection that God offers us through submission. Satan will do all he can to break us down and tear us away from God. James is making a statement here that not only yields encouragement, but also holds a warning within. Satan gains access to our hearts when we don't hold to God and try to do things on our own.

Submitting to God is far from easy. Our human nature doesn't want to give up control and put our full trust in another. However, the more you dig into God's Word, the more it is evident that complete submission to God is the best way to go.

There are a lot of ways people can live their lives, but there is only one way to Heaven. We are saved by the blood of Jesus and nothing else. God wants you and me to be in Heaven with Him when our time on Earth is through. This world may try to pull us away, but know and believe that Satan is powerless to take you away from God when you are under His wing. I hope you can see and celebrate how submission is truly a beautiful thing.

Prayer

Father, thank You for always being there for me. I ask that You guide my heart to completely submit myself to You. I know I can't defeat this world alone. You sent Jesus to do that for me, and I ask that You help me to live in a way that shows love and thanks for everything I gain through Him. In the name of my risen Savior I pray. Amen.

Personal Reflection

What is one area of your life where you demand control? How is Satan using that desire for control to weigh you down, and how could putting your trust in God impact this situation?

Day 6

God's Love

[16] For God so loved the world that he gave his one and only Son, that whoever believes in him shall not perish but have eternal life.

-John 3:16

W HAT IS LOVE? Is it those butterflies you get when you see your boyfriend or girlfriend? Is it a text that has a lot of heart emojis in it? Is love being told you are loved? Our world has a lot of different ideas about what love is. While all these displays of affection are great, today's devotion reveals how God's love is so much greater!

To put God's love into perspective, let's take a closer look at the verse above. The love of our Father in Heaven is so great that He gave up His ONLY Son so that we could inherit eternal life. For those of you who are parents, the gravity of this verse is a lot easier to understand than for those of us (like myself) who are not. Imagine being in a situation where the only way to save the world from sin was to watch your child die a horrible death on a cross. Just the mere thought of that would make most parents ill. We can be thankful that God did more than just ponder the thought. He came through for us in every way. He dealt with the agony of watching His Son die, and let's not forget who Jesus died for. He died for everyone. He died so that murderers, adulterers, rapists, and even terrorists could come to faith and enter the kingdom of Heaven. Jesus was perfect in every way. He didn't deserve to die. It is hard to grasp the thought of a parent sacrificing their perfect child so that a bunch of sinners like you and me could have a chance, but our Father in Heaven did. That is God's love. It stretches farther and wider than mankind will ever be able to imagine, and we have every reason in the world to be thankful for it.

So where does love come into breaking the chains of spiritual heart disease? Well, as you look around the world we live in, it is rather evident that there is more love for ourselves than there is for God. If we don't take the time to embrace the amazing love God has shown us, then we lose sight of who our God is and what He has done for us. A heart that embraces God's love is one that strives to express that love in every thought, word, and action. Through the sacrifice of Jesus we can see and know that our chains are broken, but we must never forget they are only broken through His perfect life, death, and resurrection. Jesus is the reason faith has immeasurable value. Embracing the love of Christ is the key to a heart that loves God and one another.

Prayer

Dear Lord, thank You for sending Your Son to die on the cross to save me from my sins. I know that I am nothing without the blood of Jesus and ask that You guide me to live every day with a heart that is dedicated to showing the love of my risen Savior. Amen.

Personal Reflection

Out of all of the blessings God has showered upon you, name just one of them. How has this blessing impacted your life?

Day 7

Faith-Based Designer Clothing

12 Therefore, as God's chosen people, holy and dearly loved, clothe yourselves with compassion, kindness, humility, gentleness and patience. 13 Bear with each other and forgive one another if any of you has a grievance against someone. Forgive as the Lord forgave you.14 And over all these virtues put on love, which binds them all together in perfect unity.

- Colossians 3:12-14

C HAPTER ONE OF this devotional is coming to an end. We have spent the last several days focusing on the danger of spiritual heart disease and the importance of a heart that seeks God. These verses from Colossians do a great job of tying together everything that is involved with having a heart that follows the Lord. A firm reality of this life is that we need God in every situation. The devil is constantly working to tear us down from every angle. A heart that seeks God is one that gives the devil less and less room to work with. As we take a look at the words above, I want to draw your attention to the verbiage the apostle Paul uses here. *Clothe* yourself with compassion, kindness, humility, gentleness, and patience. I have used words such as "embrace" to describe connectedness to God, but Paul's use of the word clothe is by far my favorite. Staying true in our faith is not just a here and there thing. It is not something one picks up and puts down. It is a state of being that believers are blessed with through the gift of the Holy Spirit. This wonderful reality that we are blessed with gives us every reason to live with a heart that gives God the glory. He has given us these spiritual clothes not only to guard us against evil, but also to keep us close to Him.

We all live in a world that is full of spiritual heart disease. This is the first chain of this book because understanding the importance of a spiritually healthy heart sets the stage for the rest of the way. Honestly evaluating the state of our hearts helps us understand there is not a chain in this book, or in your life, that can be broken alone. We are all powerless without God, but we can be thankful that we have the power to battle temptation and win through the help of the Holy Spirit. Never forget that God always has your back.

Prayer

Dear Jesus, please guide our hearts to long for You in every regard. We are powerless on our own to defeat the sin and the temptation that drags us down. Thank You for dying on the cross so that we would not be chained to this world by our sins. We ask that You guide our hearts to live for You, and we ask You to help us battle every temptation that comes our way. In Your name we pray. Amen.

Personal Reflection

After spending this chapter focusing on the importance of a Christ-focused heart, what is your top takeaway? How will applying this one thing you learned from God's Word impact your heart going forward?

Loneliness

Day 1

God Understands

18 The Lord God said, "It is not good for the man to be alone. I will make a helper suitable for him."

-Genesis 2:18

HAVE YOU EVER felt like you would end up alone? Like no one would ever love you and that there is no one in this world who would want to date or marry you? In high school, as well as in my early college years, I can remember these thoughts going through my head. I was turned down by every girl I asked out in high school. I dated a girl during my first year of college who I thought was going to be my wife, but then heartbreak came out of nowhere. It felt like I was never going to find someone.

We live in a world that preaches about finding happiness or finding the person who is perfect for you. It is all about what we do instead of what God does for us. I picked this verse from Genesis to start this chapter about loneliness because it is important for all of us to know that God understands us. He knew at creation that man would be much better off united with others than alone. God understands our needs and provides what we need. When we are lonely and wishing we had that special someone to go through life with, remember this: God has a plan to fill the void. Now, this plan might not necessarily include a spouse, but be confident in knowing that God will provide in the way He sees best. None of us know what the Lord has in mind until He does it, but there is a plan in place.

My life is a great example of how God understands our needs when it comes to companionship. I was heartbroken when my relationship ended after my freshman year of college. I went on dates after this breakup, but for the most part remained single and had a fair amount of struggles over the course of the next year and a half. However, God used that time as a single man to do some really cool stuff. He called me into lay ministry, and I started a Christian web show on YouTube. God also used me to write a yearlong daily devotional in that time. There was a reason God waited to send my fiancée into my life. He had work He wanted me to do first. God also used that time to help me grow in countless ways. He prepared me to be with the wonderful woman who I will marry in a couple of months. God's desire was not for me to be alone, but rather was to prepare me to be a more Godly boyfriend and future husband for the woman He had in mind.

As we talk about how loneliness can affect our relationships with God, I want you know and believe that God understands you. He knows what you can handle. He knows what you need, and He will provide you with what you need at the right time. I have been through periods of life when God allowed me to endure some loneliness, but I can assure you that He will use those times for your good.

Prayer

Dear Lord, thank You for understanding me and providing everything that I need. I ask that You guide my heart to see the beauty of Your plan for my life. I pray that Your will be done above all things. Amen.

Personal Reflection

Everyone has been single at some point in their lives. Has there been a time when you were single and felt that you would never find a husband or wife? How did God use that time to draw you closer to Him?

Day 2

God Is There For You

¹⁰ So do not fear, for I am with you; do not be dismayed, for I am your God. I will strengthen you and help you; I will uphold you with my righteous right hand.

-Isaiah 41:10

LONELINESS IS SOMETHING that is real and can be felt in many situations. Upon going through struggles and hardships, there may be feelings of loneliness even when there are people all around. As we dig into our devotion today, I want you to ponder this question: can we break the chain of loneliness with human interaction alone? The world would tell us we can, but can worldly companionship really shatter those heavy chains?

The verse above from Isaiah sheds light on ways that God's presence is felt. These words reveal to us that God is with His people and is there when they need Him. The reality of this passage is that God is the one who lifts us up. He is the one who is always there for us. He know when we are weak and need strength. He knows!

As we look at all the evidence of how God is there for His people, can we ever say we are alone? Is loneliness really a chain? Yes, it is, but it is different than the other ten in this book. Solitude is not a state of reality, but rather is a state of mind that our sinful nature causes us to fall into. The other chains are states of reality that take place in our lives. The challenge with loneliness is not resisting temptation that we could fall into, but rather is defeating the lie that we are alone. WE ARE NEVER ALONE! As long as you and I live, God will always be there for us. We can turn our back on Him and reject Him, but that doesn't mean He is gone (the only place where mankind is completely separated from God is Hell). God is still here, which is exactly why true solitude and loneliness on this earth are only a state of mind.

Depending on who you are, this chain may be the toughest one to break, but don't fear. God is with you and can help you break this state of mind just like anything else. The Lord is there to hear your prayer and wants to help you through every situation. He has your back and will never let you down. Always remember that you are never alone!

Prayer

Dear Father in Heaven, thank You for always being there for me. There are times that feelings of loneliness consume me and drag me down. I ask that You guide me to see that You are always ready to hear my prayers and to comfort me on my darkest day. In Jesus' name I pray. Amen.

Personal Reflection

There are many situations in life when it can be very easy to feel alone. Think of a time when you felt as if you were stuck in solitude even though you were not. Who was there for you? How were those people a positive light at that time? Also, when you look back on that time, can you see how God was there for you?

Day 3

Fear Not

⁶ The Lord is with me; I will not be afraid. What can mere mortals do to me?

-Psalm 118:6

H AVE YOU EVER felt powerless? Like there was nothing you could do to defeat the trials that this world was piling on you? Like you were trapped in a box with nothing to do but wait for the worst? Feelings of being alone can cause us to endure a lot of bothersome emotions, but I think it is safe to say that fear may be one of the strongest. Feeling alone often makes us feel vulnerable and susceptible to the attacks this world inflicts on us. While feeling hopelessly alone may seem like a normal part of life, does it have to be? Is there an attitude that mankind can hold that has the ability to defeat the fear of being alone?

Today's verse from the book of Psalms is a great example of how observing the presence of God defeats the fear within that is found in loneliness. While the exact context of this Psalm is not completely understood or agreed upon by Bible scholars, there is overwhelming evidence that this Psalm was written as a song of thanksgiving after a military battle had been won. The words above speak volumes of the faith that was placed in God in this vulnerable situation. While in battle, it can be very easy to feel alone, like it is you against the world. The words above show the powerful comfort that can be found through the presence of God in the worst of situations. The Psalm writer states, "What can mere mortals do to me?" as if a sword could have been stabbed through his heart, and he would not have feared. The presence of God gave this soldier or leader so much comfort that death did not scare him. There is no loneliness or feelings of solitude found here. Well then, what is the secret to the madness? How can someone be so confident in such a vulnerable situation? It all comes down to one word. Faith.

Today's devotion is very closely tied to others in this chapter. Again, we are reading about how God is there for us and how there is no need to fear, but today we are going to place a deeper focus on some links within this chain of loneliness that can weigh heavily on our hearts and minds. Knowing that God is there for us is one thing, but having faith in the power and authority of His presence is another. Fear is what the devil uses to make us think we are alone and that death can finish us off. This Psalm is a great example of what it means to embrace the presence of God. My encouragement for you going forward is to look at this verse and embrace the amazing comfort which is found in knowing that this world is powerless to defeat us when God is by our side.

Prayer

Dear Lord, please help me to see there is no reason to fear with You by my side. Not even death can separate me from You. Thank You for being an ever-present light in my life, and please help me to share Your light with others. Amen.

Personal Reflection

Go back in time to a place in your past when you or someone you love was in an extreme life or death situation. How was that situation handled? Was the presence of God embraced within that struggle? If not, how could you better embrace God's presence in the future?

Day 4

God Has You Covered

[25] "Therefore I tell you, do not worry about your life, what you will eat or drink; or about your body, what you will wear. Is not life more than food, and the body more than clothes? [26] Look at the birds of the air; they do not sow or reap or store away in barns, and yet your heavenly Father feeds them. Are you not much more valuable than they? [27] Can any one of you by worrying add a single hour to your life?

-Matthew 6:25-27

A S WE THINK about loneliness, there is a rather silent element of this topic that I think we can all relate to. Take a moment to think of a time when you asked God for something. Your answer could be something material such as food and clothes or could be something related to a gift or ability. Another request could be relief from anxiety that comes from the strains of life in general. An example from my personal life would be worries that came from not knowing if I would have a job after graduation. The important thing here is to think of something you really wanted God to provide or make better, or think of an experience that seemed like it had no foreseeable solution and made you feel alone. I encourage you to carry this thought with you through the rest of this devotion.

As you can probably already see based on the verses above, worrying is our topic of the day. Now I want you to take your answer to my first question and apply it to this one: how did my worries about _____ impact my feeling about God's presence in my life? Did you feel alone, afraid, or rejected when God didn't provide in the way that you wanted Him to? Did you feel like you had to figure out how to get the answer you wanted on your own? Feeling alone in these situations is something that mankind faces every day mostly due to rejecting or not trusting God. A mentality that says, "If God doesn't give me what I need, then I will just have to figure it out myself" is not only damaging to one's faith but is also completely false. Jesus demonstrates for us in Matthew 6 that we have value in His eyes. We are, without a doubt, more valuable than the birds to our Father in Heaven, and He provides them with everything they need, so is there any reason to doubt He will provide all that we need? The point here is that God will provide us with all we need in every situation. There is no need to feel alone or to think we have to figure things out on our own. God has it all figured out and will provide us with what is truly best. We only get one time of grace on this earth, and verse 27 is a great reminder of how worrying about what we do or don't have will not give us a single hour more!

Prayer
Dear Giver of all, thank You for providing me with everything I need. Please help me to never take my blessings for granted. Amen.

Personal Reflection
God provides all that we need every day of our lives. Think of one time in your life when you felt God wasn't providing what you needed? What feelings were reflected at God in this instance? How do these verses from Matthew provide comfort in knowing that God is always there for you?

Day 5

Your Light in Dark Valleys

⁴ Even though I walk through the valley of the shadow of death, I will fear no evil, for you are with me; your rod and your staff, they comfort me.

-Psalm 23:4 ESV

T HE EXPERIENCE OF life could definitely be defined as a roller coaster ride. Everyone goes through events that change the landscape from smooth and easy to bumpy and intense. This life is far from easy, but in order to hold true to our faith in a sinful world, we must never forget that we always have a soft place to land.

One of the most dangerous elements about the chain of loneliness is that our world offers remedies that claim to lighten the load, when in fact they make this chain even heavier and more suffocating. When dealing with tough situations like breakups, divorces, or deaths of loved ones, it can be much easier to turn to drinking, partying, pornography, or any number of things to fill the void of loneliness that has entered our lives. Satan places hazards in our darkest valleys so that he can get us to trip and fall. He wants us to go the worldly direction with the hope that we will turn away from the light of God.

This verse relates very well to the others we have looked at in this chapter, but there is a specific word that I want to focus in on today. Comfort. In the darkest valleys of life, God is there with us. He is there to be a light for our path to guide us as a shepherd does for his sheep. Now, all that being said, this does not mean trusting God's way of doing things is the easiest route. In fact, it may be the hardest thing to do in an extreme situation. When these kind of circumstances face you head on, my hope is that you will remember this phrase: the world offers short term solutions that fail, but God offers long term solutions and salvation that prevail.

Everyone faces dark valleys in this life that cause temptation to set in. In those times of doubt and struggle, never forget there is no reason to fear because God loves you and is there to comfort you in every stage of your life.

Prayer

Dear God, thank You for being there for me in my darkest valleys. I ask that You guide me to see the light of Your love. Please help me to embrace the comfort You so readily provide in every tough situation. Amen.

Personal Reflection

All of us have those dark times in our lives when it may seem like all hope is lost. Go back to that point in time when you were in a dark valley, and evaluate how you handled that situation. Did you look to God for comfort? Did you look elsewhere? What have you learned, and how can you better embrace the love and comfort of God when tough times come in your future?

Day 6

You Are Part of the Body

¹² Just as a body, though one, has many parts, but all its many parts form one body, so it is with Christ. ¹³ For we were all baptized by one Spirit so as to form one body—whether Jews or Gentiles, slave or free—and we were all given the one Spirit to drink. ¹⁴ Even so the body is not made up of one part but of many.

-1 Corinthians 12:12-14

WERE YOU THE kid who was picked first to be on the team at recess, or last? Were you the student who got an A on just about everything, or were you struggling to get a C? It seems like no matter what realm of life we look at, we are all categorized by our gifts and talents. This world is often very good at labeling people with identifiers such as smart, dumb, athletic, nerdy, wealthy, poor, gifted, and so on. As I look back at my childhood, I would say that I had mixed experiences when it came to how I was viewed in sports and in school. There were moments I would catch a touchdown pass, and there were other times I would punt the football backwards over my head and manage to get negative yardage on a punt. I can remember those moments of feeling useless in my childhood as I am sure you can. Those moments when it feels like your gifts and talents are useless can be devastating and yes, even lonely.

Today is all about digging into how we are never alone because of the awesome team we are a part of. The verses above from 1 Corinthians reveal to us how we are all part of the body of Christ. All people of faith are an active piece. There are no bench warmers, and everyone is a critical part of the team. Everyone has the ability to be a key player thanks to the captain who is our Father in Heaven. God has given each of His people very unique and special gifts to use when it comes to serving His kingdom. It is easy to say we are all an equally important piece of the body of faith. However, this reality may not be so easy to believe, especially when we feel like our gifts are useless, and we feel alone. Despite how we may feel at times, these verses from 1 Corinthians provide comfort in many ways. Not only can we find joy in the fact that God is using us to serve His kingdom, but we can also give thanks for the community of faith that is ours through the gift of the Holy Spirit. There are churches, Bible studies, youth nights, and so many other opportunities for us to be connected with members of the body of Christ. There is no doubt God blesses us richly through Christian communities, and we can always give thanks that through faith we are never alone!

Prayer

Dear Lord, thank You for making me part of Your body through faith. I am often tempted to think that I am alone and that my gifts are no good. I ask that You help me to see the beauty in all of the gifts and talents You have showered upon me. Amen.

Personal Reflection

Think of a time in your past when your gifts and talents seemed useless to the point where you felt left out. Now, pick out three gifts that God has given you. How can you use these gifts to serve Him and the body of Christ?

Day 7

You Are Never Alone!

¹⁶ And I will ask the Father, and he will give you another advocate to help you and be with you forever—¹⁷ the Spirit of truth. The world cannot accept him, because it neither sees him nor knows him. But you know him, for he lives with you and will be in you.

-John 14:16-17

T HE WORDS ABOVE are probably not considered some of the most popular in the Bible. However, these verses do hold an amazing truth. For our final devotion on the chain of loneliness, I want to dig into these two verses about the gift of the Holy Spirit. On the surface, these words may not seem to fall in line with what we have talked about in this chapter. However, in my opinion these words hold the most comfort of them all!

The verses above from the gospel of John were spoken by Jesus as words of comfort to His disciples. These devout followers of Jesus were used to having Him right by their side. They were able to learn directly from Jesus about how to love God and to serve others. As you can probably imagine, the thought of Jesus leaving may not have seemed all that great at the time, but remember this: Jesus came to live perfectly, suffer, die, and rise again so that all would have the hope of eternal life in Heaven. His mission on this earth was complete, and it was time for the disciples to serve God's kingdom through the same means, but in a different form. When Jesus says, "for He lives with you and will be in you," He is talking about the presence of the Holy Spirit in the hearts of the disciples. Jesus may not be on this earth today, but God is with us through the gift of the Holy Spirit. The Holy Spirit lives within the hearts of all who have faith in our risen Savior, Jesus. We are never alone because God lives in us!

Out of all of the topics you will read about in this devotional, loneliness may be the hardest to get a full grasp on. As I mentioned earlier in the chapter, this chain is different because it is not a reality like all of the others but rather is a falsified state of mind that the devil tempts us to fall into. God loves you. He will always be there for you, and you can always be assured that even in the deepest and darkest moments of life, you are never alone.

Prayer

Dear Jesus, thank You for coming into this world to save me from my sins. I had no hope without You, but do have the greatest hope of Heaven thanks to You! Please use the Holy Spirit to give me comfort when I feel alone and afraid. Guide me to see how You work all things out for my good. In Your name I pray. Amen.

Personal Reflection

Through faith, the Holy Spirit lives in your heart every day. Think of a time recently when you felt alone in a situation where you could have talked about Jesus with others, but didn't. How can remembering the presence of God within you give comfort when another opportunity to witness to others comes up in the future?

3

Complexity

Day 1

Setting Your Focus

12 Salvation is found in no one else, for there is no other name
under heaven given to mankind by which we must be saved."

-Acts 4:12

W<small>HO OR WHAT</small> is your god? A question like this may seem borderline offensive to a Christian, but I really want you to think about it. Think about the tasks that consume your day. The effort you put into grooming yourself to look better than ever. The time you give to your career and the extra hours you put in so that you can drive a nicer car or buy a bigger house. Think about the dedication you have for extracurricular activities such as sports and clubs. Consider the time you put into texting your friends to keep in touch and stay connected. All of these things and many more grab our attention and consume our focus. Everything listed above has potential to be good, but does there come a point when they become bad?

Now that you have thought about all of the elements of your day that consume your focus, I want to ask you this question: how much of your daily focus is dedicated to God? When I ask myself this question, I am often ashamed if I am being completely honest. I spend so much of my day focused on my career, running my business and completing school work that I don't seem to have much time for God. I love the Lord and strive to live for Him every day, but it is hard to say that my focus on Him is at the level it could or should be.

If you and I are honest, we know that we allow the complex world we live in to be more complex than it really is. We live in a time when our world is ever changing and always moving. The truth is that we have little power to change how the world operates, but we do have the will to choose how we embrace it. This verse from the book of Acts is a great reminder of why a primary focus on God is crucially important. This world will tempt us to think that possessions and improved abilities through hard work will help us achieve joy and happiness. While it is true that we may find some temporary satisfaction in those things, they have little value compared to what our Savior offers. Only through faith in Jesus are we saved. Money, a fit body, or worldly knowledge will not attain us the true joy that is everlasting life in Heaven.

Our world is very complex and has a lot of working parts, but I want to challenge you to do something I have challenged myself to do every day for the last couple of years. Set aside a piece of time and dedicate your focus completely to God. Talk to Him. Read His Word and embrace His love. I am confident that you will be amazed how even a little focused time with God every day can lead to a lifestyle that embraces the salvation that is only found in Christ alone.

Prayer

Dear Jesus, my life is complex and my attention is pulled in many different directions. You are my Savior, and I want to dedicate my focus and my life to showing You love. I love You Lord and ask that You help me to place my primary focus on You. In Your name I pray. Amen.

Personal Reflection

Think of a five to ten minute period during the day when you could completely dedicate yourself to time with God. What could you do with this time, and how can you make this a daily event?

Day 2

A Simple Diet

35 Then Jesus declared, "I am the bread of life. Whoever comes to me will never go hungry, and whoever believes in me will never be thirsty.

-John 6:35

HOW LONG DO you spend looking at the menu when you go out to eat? For me, I can normally pick out something that sounds really good rather fast. However, I have a mother who makes a restaurant menu look like a dictionary from time to time. My mom is the furthest thing from a picky eater, but she does like to be aware of what just about every item on the menu is before she makes her decision. At a nice restaurant, the task of choosing something to eat off of a large and complex menu can be a little intimidating (even for me). Today's devotion is all about how deciding on our spiritual food is a much simpler task.

As you look at the verses above, the concept that Jesus lays before us seems very straightforward, but is it easy? Don't get me wrong, saying that Jesus is the way to eternal life rolls right off the tongue for most Christians. Now comes the hardest question of the day: is applying this principle to our lives as easy as saying it? Are we dedicated to a life that says Jesus is number one, or do we seek fullness in our jobs, possessions, hobbies, and relationships that only the bread of life (Jesus) can provide? If we are being completely honest with each other, we know we have all fallen short. We have all went after bread that looked a lot tastier in the short term than the bread of life that gives salvation. How can we possibly give our full attention to the bread of life in a world that is extremely complex with so many options and choices? There are probably a lot of ways theologians would answer this question, but I want to break it down to one name. The Holy Spirit.

As we go through this life and strive to stay focused on the bread of life, it is important to always remember that you have the gift of the Holy Spirit in your heart. This world may tempt you with a lot of unholy food like drugs, alcohol, and porn that promise a full feeling. Regardless of the temptation to embrace those temporary highs, we can feel secure knowing that God is working in us. His Spirit is there to guide us in our weakest moments.

Our lives will likely only get more complex. Our world is changing at a fast rate, and it appears that the rate of change will only get faster. Despite the changes and all the complex issues we live with every day, may we never forget to keep things simple by always seeking the bread of life above everything else!

Prayer

Dear Jesus, please help me to seek You above all material things, relationships, and situations. The world makes countless claims about ways that I can be filled, but I know there is only one. Please guide my heart to serve You only. Amen.

Personal Reflection

Think of something or someone in our world that claims to offer a fullness that only God can provide. How have you been tempted by this source, and how can you better seek God to help you through a similar situation in the future?

Day 3

Seek Him First

[33] But seek first his kingdom and his righteousness, and all these things will be given to you as well. [34] Therefore do not worry about tomorrow, for tomorrow will worry about itself. Each day has enough trouble of its own.

-Matthew 6:33-34

W HAT ARE YOUR priorities, or in other words, what are the most important things in your life? For me, my relationship with God is number one. From there, I would have to say that Sarah (my fiancée) is second, then my family, and so on. Over time I have noticed it is really easy to say that my top two priorities are God and family, in that order. However, it is clear that my heart does not always follow my words. It's not that I don't want God to be first, but it is really hard to achieve. Maybe you can relate? Complexity is perhaps a chain that Satan uses now more than ever before in human history, and we really can't deny it.

We are extremely busy in 21st century America trying to fit 12 activities into a 10 slot schedule. A great example of this would be my fiancée and I planning our wedding. For any of you who have gotten married or have helped a friend with wedding planning, you know exactly how much is involved with preparing for that day. It is not always stressful, but the complexity involved with planning a wedding in our culture is often extreme. The hall and the church need to get booked. Invitations, decorations, honeymoon planning, parties, and showers demand hours upon hours of time. On top of the planning, there are worries and concerns about the "what ifs" when thinking about the weather that could come with a December wedding in Wisconsin. There are so many working parts and lots of things that can be worried about. As you can see from this example in my life, it is really easy to let the complexity of a situation get the best of you and make you worry about what is out of your control.

When it comes down to it, we all have periods in our lives when our full schedules draw us away from seeking God first. This may happen to you only once in a while, or it may happen to you on an hourly basis. Regardless of your situation, never forget that seeking God first is truly best. Only through Jesus can salvation be found, and only through Him can we have peace. There are a million things we can worry about in our efforts to achieve everything on our to-do list. That being said, never forget that the next hour, day, week, month, and year will worry about itself. God has everything under control, which means we have a prime opportunity to seek Him first here and now.

Prayer

Dear Father, at times my life gets so loaded down with tasks that it is hard to find time for You. Please help me to let tomorrow worry about itself so I can focus more on You today. Amen.

Personal Reflection

What is one element of your life that you often seek before God? Pray about this and ask God to help you put Him first in this area of your life.

Day 4

Complexity's Fall

² I am jealous for you with a godly jealousy. I promised you to one husband, to Christ, so that I might present you as a pure virgin to him.³ But I am afraid that just as Eve was deceived by the serpent's cunning, your minds may somehow be led astray from your sincere and pure devotion to Christ. ⁴ For if someone comes to you and preaches a Jesus other than the Jesus we preached, or if you receive a different spirit from the Spirit you received, or a different gospel from the one you accepted, you put up with it easily enough.

-2 Corinthians 11:2-4

D O YOU KNOW someone who has fallen away from God? Someone who knew and believed in Jesus as their Savior, but then tossed Him aside to follow another culture or religion? Or maybe this person completely gave up on the idea of a deity all together and believes that there is no God. I have heard very sad stories of people falling away, but I am fortunate to be able to say I have never experienced this on a personal level with people who are close to me. The reality of our world is that there are lots of false gods out there. There are many religions and practices that may even claim to worship the one true God, but in reality use this line to lure people into lies. Today's devotion is all about keeping things simple in a world that makes religion, and even Christianity, very complex.

To dive into this topic even deeper, let's look at an example from the Bible of someone who was concerned about the faith of others. The verses above are from a letter that the apostle Paul wrote to the church of Corinth. These few verses state very clearly the concerns that Paul had about the people of his church being tempted by those who did not worship the true God. While the language of these verses is not in a form we commonly use in the current time, it really drives home how serious this situation was. For instance, verse two uses the word "virgin" to state how the hearts of these Christians were pure and solely focused on the true God, but then verse three tells us how the people were being tempted and were falling just as Eve was tempted in the Garden of Eden. The final verse of this section states Paul's concerns about how the people of Corinth were allowing these false teachings to impact their faith and invade their hearts. They were not standing firm, and this was a scary situation just as it would be if our loved ones were falling away.

The topic of this devotion is very loaded and, quite frankly, is depressing to talk about, so why do it? This world is full of different religions, cults, and spiritual practices that preach something other than salvation that is found through faith in Jesus. Above anything that you could take away from this devotion, my hope is that you zero in on your faith in Jesus as your Savior and block out false prophets.

Prayer
Dear Lord, please guide my heart to You and You only. Amen.

Personal Reflection
Think of a time in your life when you were tempted to believe in something other than God's Word. How did you respond, and what could you do to better avoid those kinds of situations in the future?

Day 5

Focus on Your Need

[38] As Jesus and his disciples were on their way, he came to a village where a woman named Martha opened her home to him. [39] She had a sister called Mary, who sat at the Lord's feet listening to what he said. [40] But Martha was distracted by all the preparations that had to be made. She came to him and asked, "Lord, don't you care that my sister has left me to do the work by myself? Tell her to help me!" [41] "Martha, Martha," the Lord answered, "you are worried and upset about many things, [42] but few things are needed—or indeed only one. Mary has chosen what is better, and it will not be taken away from her."

-Luke 10:38-42

HOW DO YOU serve Jesus in your daily life? Do you serve your church by cutting the lawn or folding bulletins? Do you show love for Jesus and others by doing maintenance work or cleaning your church? Maybe you serve as a Sunday school teacher or do lay ministry. Now that you had a chance to think about how you serve, I want to ask you a reflective question. How does the way you serve impact your relationship with God? The question here is not about whether what we are doing is good or not because serving God is good. The question is: are there times we could be doing something better?

As we look at the verses above from the book of Luke, we can probably visualize ourselves in the shoes of Martha. Can you even imagine having the Son of God in your home? I would be a nervous wreck if I had to make that guy dinner! It is easy for us to understand how Martha got so tied up in the details that she forgot about her genuine *need*. Jesus used this instance with Mary and Martha as a great opportunity to show how spiritual needs are so much more valuable than any physical or "convenient" needs. It would appear absolutely necessary in that situation to cook up a good meal for Jesus. I think we can both say that would be high on our priority list, but the point made here is one that we should carry with us every day.

The truth is that we have no greater need than the need we have for Jesus. In our case, Jesus is the difference between eternal life and eternal death. His life, death, and resurrection punched our ticket to Heaven. When it comes down to it, Jesus is all that we truly need! He is our amazing Savior who cared enough about sinners like us to suffer a horrible death to pay the price for our sins. We are nothing without Him.

There will be times now and in the future when we will be tempted to serve God in a way that actually distracts us from what is really important. Serving the Lord and being involved at church are awesome things to do, but never forget to stop and take in the wisdom that only comes from the words of our amazing God.

Prayer

Dear Jesus, please help me to seek time with You. I love serving You but often let my complex lifestyle draw me away from my spiritual needs. Please guide my heart to seek my true need. Amen.

Personal Reflection

Think of a time when you put forth your effort to serve God but did not really listen to what He had to say. How could you better embrace the Word of God in the future?

Day 6

Rest on the Spirit

2 And so it was with me, brothers and sisters. When I came to you, I did not come with eloquence or human wisdom as I proclaimed to you the testimony about God. ² For I resolved to know nothing while I was with you except Jesus Christ and him crucified. ³ I came to you in weakness with great fear and trembling. ⁴ My message and my preaching were not with wise and persuasive words, but with a demonstration of the Spirit's power, ⁵ so that your faith might not rest on human wisdom, but on God's power.

-1 Corinthians 2:1-5

H OW DO YOU feel about evangelism? As Christians, we can all say with confidence that spreading the gospel of Jesus is extremely important. But when it comes down to sharing the Word with someone one on one, do our feelings tend to change a little? I know for me, talking about my faith with others is a work in progress. I am passionate about sharing the amazing truth of Jesus with others, but there are still times when I am fearful of entering a situation where I may not know the answer to a question. Just the thought of trying to know the answers to every Jesus question boggles my mind and makes me frustrated from time to time. Maybe you can relate. The verses above not only demonstrate how we are able to respond to questions about our faith but also give some perspective on who we should trust when we have questions.

If you are someone who watches the evening news, you have probably seen a few crazy stories in recent years about preachers who have made outrageous but yet persuasive claims about things that God has enabled them to do. In situations like this, it can be hard to decipher who is speaking the truth and who is filling you with lies. This element of Christianity can make things seem very complex when they are indeed quite simple. So, how can we see who is telling the truth? This answer could be displayed several ways but has two core elements: the Holy Spirit and the Bible.

As you live, share, and embrace the love of Jesus in your life, always remember that you are never alone when it comes to witnessing for Him. The Holy Spirit is present in your heart and will guide you to that right answer. Also, always remember that Godly wisdom is found and obtained through Scripture. Studying the Word of God is a great defense against all of the false teachers who put a twisted spin on God and what He is about. We can have peace through Scripture and confidence through the gift of the Holy Spirit. God is with us and will provide answers to the questions on our minds in His perfect timing.

Prayer

Dear Lord, faith can seem so complex. There are times when I don't know how to answer questions about You, and others when I question the teachings of pastors and preachers. Please give me peace through the gift of Your Spirit and guide me to be a strong example of what it means to follow You. Amen.

Personal Reflection

Our world has a lot of false teachers and is full of questions about Christianity. How can we find peace in this struggle?

Day 7

The Law Made Simple

35 One of them, an expert in the law, tested him with this question: 36 "Teacher, which is the greatest commandment in the Law?" 37 Jesus replied: "'Love the Lord your God with all your heart and with all your soul and with all your mind.' 38 This is the first and greatest commandment. 39 And the second is like it: 'Love your neighbor as yourself.' 40 All the Law and the Prophets hang on these two commandments."

-Matthew 22:35-40

D OES GOD'S LAW frustrate you? That may seem like an out of place question to answer when talking about Scripture, but really think about it. Do you ever get mad at yourself because you keep on failing God no matter how hard you try? It's not that you want to hurt your Father in Heaven in any way, but it just seems like there is always something that you are doing wrong. Maybe it feels like there is always a coffee table that you are tripping over no matter how hard you try to avoid it. To close out this chapter, we are going to dig deep and answer the question: what is the best way to can honor God?

Over the course of my lay ministry, I have often struggled with trying to figure out how to present God's Law. The Law serves as a curb (to keep us on track), a guide (to reveal what God desires for our lives), and a mirror (to show us our sins). Each Law of God shows us those three things, but it does not make the Law any simpler, at least until you get to Matthew 22. Jesus provides for us the sum of the Law in a form that displays a simple guideline for all Christians. Before Jesus paid for the sins of the world, the Law was in place so that God's people could maintain a right relationship with Him. Now that Jesus has paid the price and earned that right relationship with God for us, we still observe the Law and honor it, but in a different light. Obeying

God's Law (works) is not the ticket to Heaven. Rather, loving others in how we observe the Law shows God love on behalf of what Jesus has done for us. The Law is very simple because it is not about obeying every law perfectly to make sure God still loves you. If we pour our hearts into loving God and loving others, obeying the Law will come naturally. This does not mean we should ignore the Old Testament and toss out the laws we don't like. Rather, this principle from Jesus presents us an opportunity to embrace His amazing love in how we observe the truths found in the Bible. The Law may be very complex on the surface, but we can be thankful every day that Jesus came to pay the price so that it would become very simple.

Prayer

Dear Father in Heaven, I strive to live every day in a way that honors You. Please guide me to follow Your Law out of love for You and my neighbor. Please help me not to be drained by observing the Law, but rather guide me to embrace the grace that is mine through Your Son. In Jesus' name I pray. Amen.

Personal Reflection

Many Christians in our world often get caught up in pointing out what others are doing wrong. As a community of believers, how can we do a better job of loving others instead of condemning them?

4

Anxiety

Day 1

God's Got Your Back

⁷ Cast all your anxiety on him because he cares for you.
                                                        -1 Peter 5:7

W HERE IS ANXIETY present in your life? Is it a struggle that you face on a daily basis? Do you have a son or daughter who is struggling with clinical anxiety or is just struggling through the pains of growing up? Maybe you have some friends who are often anxious or struggle with confidence. Regardless of who you are, the odds are pretty good that anxiety is part of your life in some way, shape, or form. If we are being honest, we all have probably faced some sort of anxiety at some point in our own lives. Living in a sinful world that is actively trying to pull us away from God can cause anxiety. This chapter may be tough for some of you, but my hope is that you walk away from it feeling encouraged and empowered through the Holy Spirit working in your heart.

If you grew up in a Christian home, these words from 1 Peter may put together one of the first Bible verses you ever learned. These words are powerful and give direction in times when we are seeking peace. They assure us of the fact that we are not alone and that God is ready to lift our burdens from us. However, I think it is fair to say our world has minimized these words because of the amount of clinically diagnosed anxiety that exists. For some, there are chemical imbalances within the brain that make it hard to flee anxiety. Without medication, it can be hard for some to even face the world around them without trembling with a burdened heart. For those of you who know the pain of anxiety on a clinical level, be assured that God is with you and knows your pain.

When any of us face a struggle in our lives, it can be easy to look at passages in the Bible and feel condemned. Believe it or not, Satan can actually use Scripture to make us question God's love. If you struggle with anxiety, these words may look like God is making anxiety sound plain and simple when for you it is actually really difficult and complex. Satan wants our hearts to be stirred with a vicious cycle of anxiety and guilt and wants us to focus on the Law when we really need to hear and embrace the Gospel. As you work through the rest of this chapter on anxiety, my hope is that you will keep our passage from today on your heart as a guide. That being said, I also want to encourage you to embrace the amazing grace, love, and peace that is found in Jesus. Don't feel guilty about being anxious. Rather, live in the light knowing that your sins are forgiven and strive to cast your anxiety on Jesus.

Prayer

Dear God, please help me to cast my anxiety on You when things get tough. I love You and ask that You fill me with Your presence in times when it is hard to trust You. Amen.

Personal Reflection

Anxiety is a hot topic in our world today. Millions of people suffer from clinical anxiety and may struggle to see the love of God in these tough times. How can you be a better witness to those with anxiety? What Gospel passages could you share to lift feelings of defeat and guilt that anxiety often causes?

Day 2

A Perfect Plan

⁴ The word of the Lord came to me, saying,
⁵ "Before I formed you in the womb I knew you,
before you were born I set you apart;
I appointed you as a prophet to the nations."
⁶ "Alas, Sovereign Lord," I said, "I do not know how to speak; I
am too young."

-Jeremiah 1:4-6

D O YOU EVER question God's plan for your life? This question and concept is one that I have struggled with for a long time. I talked about my struggles with trusting God's plan a little in chapter one, but now I want to take you a step deeper into my struggle. In recent months, there have been a lot of questions on my mind about how God is going to use me to serve Him. I have constantly been searching for answers in terms of what God wants me to be doing. Does He want me to serve more at church? Does He want me to keep writing books? Does He want me to do ministry full-time or part-time? I don't know what He wants me to do and as much as I wish I did, I know that His answer for me might push me out of my comfort zone. This area of my life causes me to be very anxious at times. That being said, I want you to ask yourself the question: how has anxiety affected your response to God's calling for your life?

As we dig into these verses from Jeremiah, it is easy for just about anyone to understand how Jeremiah was a little anxious about his situation. In this section, God is calling Jeremiah to be the leader of His people. That is no small job, and it is hard to even imagine being given such a large responsibility directly from God. Despite the call that God has extended to you, you can probably relate to Jeremiah's answer in verse six. It can be really easy to think it is okay or acceptable to deny

God's plan because we don't have the words or wisdom to represent Him well. This train of thought may seem logical, but we can't forget that God is with us in every situation. There is not one task or calling that God will extend to you without the guidance to fulfill it. Despite the fear, doubt, and anxiety that Jeremiah was probably feeling in that moment, God was going to empower him to serve His people with dignity and wisdom.

When the opportunity comes about to serve God and those around you, my encouragement is to be confident through faith. God will always be with you just like He was with Jeremiah. He will empower you to serve well and will bless your efforts. May God be with you and give you confidence as you strive to carry out His calling for your life.

Prayer

Dear God, please help me to embrace Your plan for my life. It can be very scary to serve You in a way that is unfamiliar or uncomfortable for me. Help me to reach outside of my comfort zone and to follow the path that You have laid for me. In Jesus' name I pray. Amen.

Personal Reflection

Think of a time when you felt a nudge to serve God in some way. How did you respond to this opportunity? If you tried to ignore it, how could you better embrace opportunities to serve God and those around you in the future?

Day 3

Resist Resistance

1 The word of the Lord came to Jonah son of Amittai: ² "Go to the great city of Nineveh and preach against it, because its wickedness has come up before me." ³ But Jonah ran away from the Lord and headed for Tarshish. He went down to Joppa, where he found a ship bound for that port. After paying the fare, he went aboard and sailed for Tarshish to flee from the Lord.

-Jonah 1:1-3

T HE STORY OF Jonah is a pretty popular piece of Scripture. If you have read the story, then you know how it goes. After Jonah fled and boarded the ship to Tarshish, a great storm came and made the seas almost impossible to sail. Eventually Jonah was thrown into the sea, and the Lord provided a fish that swallowed him and protected him for three days. This is one of those pieces of Scripture that sounds like something out of a fictional movie, but that's not the case. We get to see here how God had a plan for Jonah. A plan that was not going to go unfulfilled, even if it meant keeping Jonah in a fish for a few days! As we go through our devotion today, I want you to reflect on instances from your past when you just wanted to run away from God's calling for your life.

Looking at these verses makes me think of my own attitude back in high school. I had the privilege of attending a Christian high school and was encouraged to enter ministry. The encouragement was positive and enlightening, but I chose to take it as pushy and demanding so I could get my way. I left high school wanting nothing to do with ministry, and then a few years later it happened. God called me into ministry through a web show and then through writing and public speaking. I didn't want to do those things at the time God started to extend that call, but my life is an example of how God's plan will always take precedence over our own.

As you look at the story of Jonah and even my story, you may feel a little anxious about how God works. Basically, God will use us in the way that He feels is best. You may be thinking: *so, are you telling me that I don't have control?* Yes, I am, and here is why this fact is so amazing. You don't want to have the control. Believe me! God's plan for our lives is way better than our own. If the last five years of my life would have gone according to my plan, I can safely say that things would not have turned out nearly as well as God's plan did. Our Father in Heaven knew what He was doing when He drew up the plans for our lives. It may make us a little uneasy and take us out of our comfort zones, but trust me when I say that God's plan is best. The unknowns of life may seem scary, but I want to encourage you to look to the future as a field of blessings that God will reveal to you in His time.

Prayer

Dear Father in Heaven, please help me to see the beauty in Your plan for my life. The unknowns of the future make me anxious. I want to take control but know that I am in good hands with You. Guide my heart to trust You more every day. Amen.

Personal Reflection

God's plan may not always seem glamorous and good. How can you better put your trust in the Lord when things get tough? Say a prayer and ask God to help you trust His plan with a true heart today.

Day 4

Endure with Peace

⁶ Do not be anxious about anything, but in every situation, by prayer and petition, with thanksgiving, present your requests to God. ⁷ And the peace of God, which transcends all understanding, will guard your hearts and your minds in Christ Jesus. ⁸ Finally, brothers and sisters, whatever is true, whatever is noble, whatever is right, whatever is pure, whatever is lovely, whatever is admirable—if anything is excellent or praiseworthy—think about such things.

-Philippians 4:6-8

I WANT YOU TO think of one element in your life that causes anxiety. Just one. This could be a relationship, a job, or a struggle with sin. It could be anything. Now, I want to ask you another question. When is the last time you prayed about that thing in your life that makes you anxious? If I look at my own life, it is sad to say that I don't pray about my own struggle with anxiety nearly enough. There is sometimes guilt and shame attached to this element of my life that becomes a barrier between myself and God. This devotion is all about breaking down those barriers and bringing every anxious element of our lives to God's feet. He is there for us, and we need to see and know the amazing blessings that come from placing our worries before God.

The first of the three verses above is very similar to the 1 Peter 5 passage that we looked at earlier in this chapter. Being that we have already addressed how we need to lay our anxiety before God, it is time to look at the blessings that come from doing this. Verse seven does a great job of outlining what God provides for us when we lay our anxiety at His feet. He provides peace that exceeds our own understanding. Through faith we are able to experience an inner tranquility or calmness that can only be found in Jesus. When God asks us to bring our anxiety to Him, He is not doing this to make us more anxious when we struggle to do so. Rather, our Father in Heaven is seeking to provide us with amazing peace that only He can give!

To close this devotion, let's take a look at the last verse of this piece from Philippians 4. Oftentimes, we become anxious when thoughts of undesired things or events come to mind. While it may not always be easy, the apostle Paul lays out for us what we can think about to avoid anxious thoughts. For many of us, this is easier said than done, but attempting to think about what is true, noble, and right will guide our hearts to peace that is found in Christ Jesus. May God be with you as you strive to focus your mind on Him and His purpose for Your life.

Prayer

Dear Jesus, please help me to focus my heart on You when things get tough. I often think about negative elements of my life that cause me to be anxious, which leads my heart and mind away from You. Please use Your Spirit to fill me with peace that only You can provide. Amen.

Personal Reflection

In a world that is full of sin and Godlessness, it can be very hard to think positively when there are so many negatives. Write down some positive words and thoughts to keep on your mind this week that will keep your heart focused on God.

Day 5

The Present of Presence

*⁹ Have I not commanded you? Be strong and courageous. Do
not be afraid; do not be discouraged, for the Lord your God will
be with you wherever you go."*

-Joshua 1:9

A S YOU HAVE probably noticed by now, a lot of our anxiety is
sourced in a weak or failing trust in God's plan. We have talked
about God's plan for several Old Testament Christians in this chapter,
and we are going to talk about another one today. However, there is
a specific piece of encouragement within Joshua's call to lead God's
people that I want to fixate on today. Much of our focus has been
placed on why trusting God is so important. Today's devotion shifts
our attention to embracing the amazing fact that God is with us during
the entire duration of our journey.

Throughout this book you have learned a thing or two about my
personal walk with God. The path that the Lord has laid out for me
was not what I expected, which has caused me to struggle from time
to time. That being said, my journey through the down parts of life
was more of a struggle than it had to be because of one key reason: I
forgot to embrace the presence of God in my life. When going through
the tough times, there is no doubt that I have been tempted to get
mad at God rather than embrace the fact that He is right there and
ready to help. God commands us to be strong and courageous, not
because we are that great, but because He has empowered us to be
strong and courageous through His presence in our lives. There is no
part of this life that we have to fear because we are never alone! God
is by our side and will help us through the good, the bad, and the ugly.
Anxiety and worry are tools that the devil uses to convince us that we
need to figure things out on our own. There was a whole chapter

dedicated to loneliness earlier in this book to set a foundation for when other chains want to convince us that we need to act solo. We are never alone, and we never have to figure things out alone. God is with us through every step of our lives. Always remember that the present of presence never stops giving.

Prayer

Dear God, help me to feel Your presence in my life. I can get so worked up and worried when I try to live as if You are not there. Please guide me to live in a way that says I have You walking right next to me. Amen.

Personal Reflection

As you go through your day-to-day life, what do you do to remind yourself of God's presence? If you are currently lacking in this area, how can you better embrace the fact that God is with you wherever you go?

Day 6

Where Perfect Love Is Found

¹⁸ There is no fear in love. But perfect love drives out fear, because fear has to do with punishment. The one who fears is not made perfect in love.

-1 John 4:18

W HAT MAKES YOU feel loved? Do you feel the love of others when they give you a hug or put their hand on your shoulder? Do calming words give you comfort and provide a feeling of connectedness with others? Does reading the words of the Bible fill you with the love of God? When it comes to love, there are a lot of ways that it can be given or received. That being considered, how many sources of love truly exist? The world presents countless ways to give and feel love, but does this mean that these outward displays are the source? In today's devotion, we are going to dig deep into the source of love and search for a genuine cure to the chain of anxiety.

It is probably fair to say the verse above is very comforting to all of us but even more so to those of you who struggle heavily with this chain. These words from 1 John clearly differentiate love from fear. Now, I realize that fear and anxiety are slightly different, but the commonalities of these terms bring this verse into our conversation about anxiety. When it comes to the love of God, we can see through this verse that there is no uneasiness or angst associated with it. God's love is perfect in every way, and His love never fails. When we get anxious, it can be easy to question God's love, and worry that He won't come through for us in the way that we want or need Him to. For those of you who have clinical anxiety, this reality may be more real for you than the rest of us. It can be extremely hard to trust God and feel His love at times. However, we can all be uplifted by our verse for today which shows us that God's love is perfect in every way. We have no reason to fear.

When it comes to the love of God, I believe our world gives us a lot of false ideas about how His love works. For example, if something goes really wrong in our lives and we are fearful, anxious, or in despair, we often compare God's love to worldly displays of love and wonder why we don't feel His love. Understand that God's love is perfect, which makes it very different. His love is the only love that drives out fear, and His is the only love that desires for us to have eternal life with Him. The love of the Lord is not always easy to see or understand, but be encouraged by the fact that God's love lives within the heart of every believer here on Earth. Don't let this world make you anxious by telling you the lie that God does not love you. Rather, seek His love through His Word and through the encouragement of every believer in your life.

Prayer

Dear Father in Heaven, please help me to see Your love and not to be anxious when I don't understand it. Your love is the only perfect love that exists, and I am thankful that Your love is present in the hearts of all believers. In Jesus' name I pray. Amen.

Personal Reflection

Where is God's love present in your life? How can you embrace His love better when you face anxiety and fear in the week ahead?

Day 7

Fearless in Faith

*14 "Do not let your hearts be troubled. You believe in
God; believe also in me. ² My Father's house has many rooms;
if that were not so, would I have told you that I am going
there to prepare a place for you? ³ And if I go and prepare a
place for you, I will come back and take you to be with me that
you also may be where I am. ⁴ You know the way to the place
where I am going."*

-John 14:1-4

A S WE CLOSE out this chapter on anxiety, I want to put a lot of
emphasis on the greatest gift God blesses us with, which is
eternal life. Through faith in Jesus, we can all be confident that there
is a place in Heaven that was prepared ahead of time for us. This life
will be full of struggles that may lead to anxiety, but the verses above
reveal a rock-solid truth we can be confident in. Jesus came to Earth
for us. He lived perfectly, suffered, died, and rose again to secure our
place in God's Kingdom. We have it all through faith, and because we
have it all, we can be confident in times when this world strikes us with
uncertainty that may cause anxiety.

As I look at the verses above, they give me a lot of comfort when I
think about the life of my grandfather (Vern). Over the course of my
time on Earth, I have seen Grandpa go through some really tough
struggles. He has been battling heart disease longer than I have been
alive and has had his fair share of close calls. There have definitely
been times on my way home from a visit with him that I thought I
wouldn't see him again on this side of Heaven. While those thoughts
are ones that are tough to experience, there is a feeling of joy within
that sadness that only believers in Christ can truly know. A joy that
overcomes the anxiety and fear that so many face. In those touch-and-

go situations, I have always been able to live with the comfort of knowing that Grandpa will be in Heaven on that day when he doesn't answer the phone or is not in his chair at home. This does not mean that I won't be sad that he is gone because I will miss him a lot, but nothing can hinder the comfort that comes with knowing that your loved one will be with Jesus when their time on Earth is through.

This life can be very difficult. There are diseases, injuries, temptations, and seemingly endless struggles that cause us to be anxious. Due to a medical condition, you may never be able to completely overcome anxiety on this earth, but be confident in this: Jesus paid the price and has prepared a place for you in Heaven. You can be 100% certain through faith that He has done this for you, and you can live in the light of knowing that there will be no more anxiety in that most perfect place.

Prayer

Dear Jesus, thank You for preparing a place in Heaven for me. I may struggle with anxiety until the day I die, but I ask that You give me peace and comfort that lightens the load of this chain in my life. Amen.

Personal Reflection

The thought of dying is something that causes anxiety for just about everyone. How can these words from John give you peace and confidence in your life today and in your last day on this earth?

Lust

Day 1

Understand the Source

¹⁶ For everything in the world—the lust of the flesh, the lust of the eyes, and the pride of life—comes not from the Father but from the world.

-1 John 2:16

L UST IS ONE of those sins that doesn't often get a lot of coverage in sermons or devotions. The little discussion is probably not due to a lack of perceived importance but rather comes from an inability to see lust take place. Anyone can observe sins that are physical acts, but there is no way you or I can watch someone mentally having sex with the person across the room. Lust is one of those "behind the curtain" sins, which unfortunately can make it really difficult to resist. This chain may seem rather light and unimportant at times, but as we dig into discussions about this topic, it will be evident that lust has the potential to be extremely destructive to a relationship with God.

To get things rolling today, I want to take an in-depth look at this verse from 1 John. When dealing with sin, it is always good to identify the source. The verse above makes it very clear that the world is the source of lust. Always remember that every sin is sourced in the world. None of them come from God. He does not tempt us to see if we will resist temptation. This may sound like common sense to any Christian, but being real and establishing that God is on our side is important. If we don't identify where sin comes from, then there is room for Satan to tempt us to think that God is causing us to fall. I can't say enough how important it is to remember that God is not the source of any temptation that you or I face.

Now, let's focus on the true source of lust. The world. I don't know about you, but it feels like the world is tempting me to fall into lustful sins every single day. I can't even turn on network television anymore without seeing ads that are lustful in nature. We live in a world that is consumed with sin, but that doesn't mean we are bound by it. God is with us and doesn't allow us to bear more than we can handle. It may seem impossible to resist the lustful temptations that are present in our everyday lives but it truly is.

Talking about lust may be uncomfortable, but it is very important. As we go into this chapter, the importance of identifying and resisting lust is going to become very evident. This one sin that seems rather small and harmless will expose itself as a monster that can do serious damage to your relationship with God and others. All that being said, don't let this sin scare you. God has your back. He can and will help you resist any temptation if you ask Him.

Prayer

Dear Lord, please help me to resist the temptations of this world. I know You are not the source of my struggles and ask that You help me to seek You when I am weak. Please give me strength to live according to Your will. Amen.

Personal Reflection

Identify one temptation in your life that causes you to lust whether it be on TV, the computer, etc. Think of ways you can resist or avoid these temptations in the future.

Day 2

Protect His Temple

18 Flee from sexual immorality. All other sins a person commits
are outside the body, but whoever sins sexually, sins against
their own body. 19 Do you not know that your bodies are
temples of the Holy Spirit, who is in you, whom you have
received from God? You are not your own; 20 you were bought
at a price. Therefore honor God with your bodies.

-1 Corinthians 6:18-20

T HE VERSES ABOVE have served as a means of discussion for several
devotions and web shows I have done over the last few years.
When it comes to talking about and identifying the issues that lust
causes, these verses from the apostle Paul's letter to the Corinthians
really say it best. To evaluate this piece of Scripture, I am going to
break it down into two basic parts.

Lust is something that can't be seen but rather is sin that takes
place only in the heart. It can be very tempting to have the thought,
I'm not hurting anyone, so it's no big deal. However, verse 18 from
above states exactly why lust is a big deal. Sexual sins take place in the
heart and are sins that damage our own bodies. Notice how this verse
says: "All other sins a person commits are outside the body." Sexual
sins dig deep and are ones that Satan takes advantage of to an
extreme in our world. The devil knows he can tear people away from
God without the direct use of other people. Sexual sins like lust make
us very vulnerable when we keep our struggles behind closed doors.
This is exactly why it is critically important to be open and honest with
God and others about the sexual sins that are burdening our lives.

Now, let's take a look at the last two verses from this piece of
scripture. These words are the wakeup call that reveal why we have
no right to tell God *this is my body, so I can do what I want with it.*

Notice how these verses point out: "You are not your own; [20] you were bought at a price." The world will say that your body belongs to you, and you can do whatever you want with it. However, through faith we know and recognize this is not the case at all. Our souls were redeemed by Jesus when He died and rose on Easter Sunday. We could not save ourselves, but He did by being the ultimate sacrifice. While this world may try to convince you that your faith is chaining you down, you can be confident through faith that your chains are broken!

This devotion about lust has been deep and possibly hard-hitting, but these guiding words from 1 Corinthians are an essential guide that can enhance our relationships with God. Regardless of how many times we fall, we can always be confident that God will be there to lift those chains if we ask Him to help us.

Prayer

Dear God, please help me to battle this sin of lust knowing that You are there to help me all the way. I know that everything I have now and will have in eternity is because of Jesus, and I ask You to help me live every day out of love for Him. In Jesus' name I pray. Amen.

Personal Reflection

Lust is a sin that goes much deeper than the world gives it credit for. Knowing this, dig deep and ask yourself how you can honor God with your body today.

Day 3

Be Honest with Yourself

²⁷ "You have heard that it was said, 'You shall not commit adultery.' ²⁸ But I tell you that anyone who looks at a woman lustfully has already committed adultery with her in his heart.

-Matthew 5:27-28

T HE FOLLOWING QUESTION goes for guys and girls because, let's face it, we all lust. Have you ever looked at the spouse of a celebrity who just happens to be a model and thought about having sex with them? I could have beat around the bush a little bit with the wording, but I am all about being honest. There are probably very few people in the world who can say that they have never looked at the spouse of another with lustful eyes and sexual thoughts. The world will tell us it is just a part of life and it is no big deal, but is that really the case?

As we dig even deeper into the chain of lust today, we are going to make some comparisons to not only show why lust is a destructive thing but also to debunk the lies that the world tells us about this topic. As we look at these words of Jesus from the book of Matthew, we can see the implications of lust are very straightforward. Jesus makes it clear that physical adultery has the exact same implications as adultery committed in our hearts. These two things are addressed very differently by the world, but are observed in the same way by God. This may sound like a scary reality, and there is no doubt that sin is a scary and depleting thing. However, as we dig into these verses there are broader and deeper implications found within these words from Jesus. The Bible tells us that works don't save us. It is only through faith and by the grace of God found in Jesus that we have the gift of eternal life (Ephesians 2:8-9). The point I am trying to make here is that these verses line up perfectly with the general light Christians live in every day. It's not all about what we do. It's not only about how we avoid sexual immorality outside of the body but is also about how we take care of and guard our hearts out of thanks for God's grace. Jesus wasn't trying to be vicious when talking about the implications of sin. He said these words to make us aware of the damage that seemingly small sins can do to our hearts of faith. He wants us to take sin seriously and not dismiss the pitfalls that could come from it. We will all struggle at times to guard our hearts and to live out of love for Jesus, but never forget that God is there to help us through every physical and heart-based battle with temptation we will face. We are loved by our Savior, and He only wants what is truly best for us!

Prayer

Dear Heavenly Father, please guide my heart, and make me aware of all the temptations Satan throws my way. Sins of lust burden my heart many times without me even knowing it. I ask that You guide me to see these wrongs and not dismiss them. Help me to show You love with my physical body and my heart. Amen.

Personal Reflection

Looking at pictures of attractive people on TV and in magazines is part of cultures all over the world. What are some ways that you could enjoy and follow pop culture without falling into temptation?

Day 4

God Will Help You Resist

¹³ No temptation has overtaken you except what is common to mankind. And God is faithful; he will not let you be tempted beyond what you can bear. But when you are tempted, he will also provide a way out so that you can endure it.

-1 Corinthians 10:13

D O YOU EVER feel like you are bound or strapped down by sexual temptation? It's not that you don't want to escape it, but it just feels like there is no way out. If this is you, I know how you feel. I mentioned earlier in this chapter that it feels like I can't even watch network television anymore without being tempted by lustful visuals. They are everywhere. We know that the links of this chain of lust can become extremely strong if we are not careful. It can be scary to think about what could happen if those chains keep getting heavier and heavier.

The verse above doesn't just pertain to sexual temptations but to all temptation in general. God wants us to know there is no sin that can overcome us. No matter how often we are tempted or how heavy the load seems to get, we can be assured through faith that we will never be defeated. Also, take notice of the wording that the apostle Paul uses at the end of this verse: "But when you are tempted, He will also provide a way out so that you can endure it." Those are perhaps some of the most comforting words that anyone struggling with sins of any kind can hear. There is always a way out! Always! No matter how trapped you feel by the sin and temptation of lust there is always a way out!

You will notice a lot of law-based verses in this devotional as we work through different chains over the next chapters, but never forget to observe all of the grace and mercy that is found within Scripture. God loves us and wants to build us up and strengthen us in our faith. As we continue through the rest of this chapter and devotional, hold your head up knowing that God will always be there to help you endure every trial this world throws at you.

Prayer

Loving God, thank You for always being there to offer me a way out of the toughest situations. Living in a sinful world is often draining and can seem hopeless, but through faith I have confidence that this world will never defeat me. Thank You for sending Jesus to live perfectly in my place. I ask that You help me to always seek a way out of temptation and sin in honor of what He has done for me. In the name of Jesus I pray. Amen.

Personal Reflection

Think of a time in your past when temptation had you depleted to the point where you felt like there was no option but to give in. How does the verse of the day impact your thoughts on facing temptation?

Day 5

Honor Marriage

⁴ Marriage should be honored by all, and the marriage bed kept pure, for God will judge the adulterer and all the sexually immoral.

-Hebrews 13:4

F OR THOSE OF you who are dating or have dated and are now married, you know how hard it is to abide by the verse above. Saving sex until marriage is far from easy. I am engaged to a wonderful, God-fearing woman. We both hold strong to our faith and make a point of establishing faith as the pinnacle of our relationship. All that being said, do our intentions and goals make it easy for us to resist sexual temptation? Not at all! One of the biggest myths about sex and marriage is that it is far easier for Christians to save sex until marriage than it is for non-Christians. In reality, almost all human beings have sexual desires that many times are not easy to resist. I will say that the presence of the Holy Spirit in my relationship with Sarah has guided us to seek God first, but the temptation is still there.

When Sarah and I started dating, we both knew that saving sex until marriage was really important to us. Our hearts were both focused on serving the Lord from the start, and we knew that clear lines had to be established in order for us to honor God's gift of marriage. So we sat down one night and established where the clear-cut line in our physical relationship would be. As time goes on and our attraction for each other grows, we have regular conversations about how we can stay true until marriage. We are both aware that temptation will get stronger as sexual passions grow, but we also know that with God's help we can do this!

While this verse from Hebrews is concerning marriage more than anything, the implications of lust are definitely present and should be observed. Lustful passions cause dating couples to fall into temptation every day. The devil will tempt us to think our sexual desires equal true love, when in reality that is a complete lie. Sex is a gift for husbands and wives to enjoy within the confines of marriage but is not the mortar that holds a marriage together. There are many lies the world will tell us about sex and lust, but don't be fooled. Sex is a beautiful gift from God that is designed for marriage. It is not easy to wait, but never forget that God will bless your every effort to live for Him.

Prayer

Dear Lord, please help us to honor Your gift of marriage. It is so easy to fall into lustful temptations when the world is completely okay with it. We ask that You guide our hearts to look to You in times of struggle. We love You and know with true hearts that You love us. Amen.

Personal Reflection

Our world dishonors marriage in many ways. Whether you are in the dating stage or the marriage stage, think of ways in which you can honor God in your current or future marriage.

Day 6

Let the Spirit Lead

^{16} So I say, walk by the Spirit, and you will not gratify the desires of the flesh. ^{17} For the flesh desires what is contrary to the Spirit, and the Spirit what is contrary to the flesh. They are in conflict with each other, so that you are not to do whatever you want.

-Galatians 5:16-17

I F THERE IS anything we can take away from this chapter, it is that lust can be a really tough thing to shake. As we go through this life, it may seem impossible to maintain a state of mind that doesn't lust. It is so easy to do, so how can we truly break this chain? *Can* we break this chain? The reality is that this chain can be broken, but we must understand with lust, as with any struggle, we can't break the chain alone. The verse above sheds light on how important it is to walk by the Spirit and to embrace the presence of God within us.

As we take a deeper look into the verses for today, it becomes more evident how we are able to endure sexual temptations. These words from Paul's letter to the Galatians talk about the conflict taking place between the Spirit of God within us and our sinful flesh. Through faith our sinful flesh is held to some terms of control. Most people would look at the description above as one of conscience, but there is more to it than that. God provides the ability to tolerate the world around us and to live for Him. Human beings have no ability to serve God without the presence of faith. It is only through the presence of God within us that we can resist temptation in a manner that shows God love.

We are all at battle with our flesh. There will be conflicts going on within our minds every day because of sin. That may sound scary, but don't be alarmed. The conflict going on inside of you and me is a good thing. The Holy Spirit is working within us through faith to guide our hearts in the right direction. Lust is a temptation that hits the battlefield of our spiritual lives for some more than others, but don't lose heart when you fall short. Jesus won the ultimate prize of Heaven for all believers. He just wants us to keep trying and to know we are not in this battle alone.

Prayer

Dear Holy Spirit, thank You for being present to help me fight battles with temptation every day. There are times I feel defeated and lost. Please comfort me when struggles come, and build me up to be a strong and faithful ambassador for You. Amen.

Personal Reflection

Think of a time when you felt defeated and lost, like there was no way you could resist a temptation. After reading the verses from today's devotion, how will you observe temptation in the future?

Day 7

A Prayer for Strength

¹⁰ Create in me a pure heart, O God, and renew a steadfast spirit within me.

-Psalm 51:10

T HIS VERSE FROM the book of Psalms is my favorite prayer for times when the temptation of lust is hitting me hard. You probably didn't have to read this chapter to know that a sin like lust can be really hard to resist. However, my hope is that you were able to take away some great guidelines from God's Word about what lust is, why it is dangerous, and how it can indeed be resisted. Satan does his best to throw a lot of curveballs our way and does anything and everything he can to get us to fall. One of the keys to resisting temptation is not only knowing God is there to help, but continually reading the Bible and staying connected to Him through prayer is critically important.

As you go through your day-to-day life in the coming weeks, I encourage you to hold this prayer for purity close to your heart. Read these words again and memorize them if that helps you to keep them on your mind. This prayer is very short, but yet is very powerful. This verse from Psalms is not only asking for a pure heart but is also asking for a renewed spirit and a re-established focus on God. These words have power and are very direct in how they ask for help with the *heart* and *spirit*. It has been mentioned more than once in this chapter that lust is a heart problem. We need our Father in Heaven to work on our hearts and to help us focus on Him.

This devotion ends our study about the chain of lust, but my encouragement for you is to carry what you have learned with you through the rest of this book and beyond. Carry the words of the verses we studied this week with you. Plant them on your heart, and continually ask God to guide your body and mind to love and serve

Him. You and I may be powerless to break this chain alone, but through the blood of Jesus we can live every day knowing that any and every chain can be broken.

Prayer

Dear God, thank You for always being there for me. There are times when my heart gets weighed down with struggles, and I feel defeated to my core. I ask that You guide me to look to You when times get tough. Please create in me a pure heart, O God, and renew a steadfast spirit within me. Amen.

Personal Reflection

Go back to a time when your heart was crushed by dirty thoughts and shame. Use that visual to think of instances in the future when you can readily use our verse from today as a prayer.

6

Envy

Day 1

Spiritual Decay

30 A heart at peace gives life to the body, but envy rots the bones.

-Proverbs 14:30

E NVY, JEALOUSY, CONCEITED desires, wanting other people's stuff. On the surface, it seems like there is nothing wrong with desiring what we don't have. The world teaches us to have wishful desires based on what the wealthy and famous have. There are a lot of attitudes that say we are entitled to certain possessions and have a right to certain benefits. Too many times we are taught there is no reason you or I shouldn't have it all. To start this chapter about the chain of envy, I want to ask you a question: what do you deserve? Keep that question in mind as we dig into our devotion today and return to it as you read through the chapter.

The verse above uses some pretty graphic imagery, doesn't it? "Envy rots the bones." Those sound like some pretty serious implications. However, upon looking at more scriptural evidence aside of this Proverb, you will quickly notice that the wording used here is pretty accurate. If I were to ask you: what is the biggest issue with envy, what would you say? Some common answers might be: "envy causes me to sin against my neighbor" or "jealous attitudes misrepresent who I am as a Christian." Answers like those are correct, but they don't address the deep underlying issue that is present with envy. This sin has the potential to damage your relationship with God as if your bones were rotting, and here is why. God is the provider of all. He gives us everything we need to live, breath, and sustain our bodies. When we fix our eyes on the possessions of others, we are forgetting, or maybe even denying, that God will and can provide us with everything we need. We need our Father in Heaven and need to acknowledge that He is our ultimate provider. We NEED Him, and we know through faith that we are nothing without Him.

This first devotion on envy is pretty hard-hitting, but it sets the pace for the rest of the chapter. Before we can truly dig into and expose the weaknesses found within the chain of envy, it is good to understand what it is capable of. As I said before, we need God! We are nothing without Him. My encouragement for you going through these devotions is to remember the central truth that no chain is ever broken without the help of God. He has your back and is ready to help you.

Prayer

Dear Lord, please guide my heart to seek You in every situation. I am often tempted to think that I need the possessions and relationships of others. You know my needs perfectly, and I ask that You help me to seek You and not to selfishly seek what others have. In Jesus' name I pray. Amen.

Personal Reflection

Identify one possession, relationship, or ability that someone has that you wish you had. Now, think of a possession, relationship, or ability that God has graciously given you. How can you use that one thing to serve Him? Also, when is the last time you thanked God for this blessing in your life?

Day 2

Just Ask

4 What causes fights and quarrels among you? Don't they come from your desires that battle within you? ² You desire but do not have, so you kill. You covet but you cannot get what you want, so you quarrel and fight. You do not have because you do not ask God. ³ When you ask, you do not receive, because you ask with wrong motives, that you may spend what you get on your pleasures.

-James 4:1-3

HAVE YOU EVER wanted something so bad that you would have done anything to get it? Maybe a fight with a sibling over a toy during your childhood comes to mind. Or maybe there is a house, car, boat, experience, or relationship that you would seemingly give anything to have. Think of that one thing that has extreme value to you, and keep it in mind. Now, I want you to dig deep and ask yourself: have you ever asked God for that thing you want?

As I think back on my time in high school, I can clearly remember my deep desire to have a girlfriend. With the exception of a few months, I was single during my high school years. There is no doubt that I was very frustrated with not being able to find someone who I could date. That being said, when I really think about that time, I can't say I remember praying about my struggle very often, if even at all. As we look at the verses above from the book of James, we can see a clearly stated warning of what envy can do to us. There is nothing wrong with desiring a relationship or a possession of some sort, but these words show us how out of hand things can get when we don't seek God with our desires. Words like "kill" and "fight" may seem extreme but are they really? The truth is that we live in a world where people fight, and yes, even kill others because they are consumed by envy. The reality of this chain is very dark indeed, but never forget the point of these verses. God is always there for us and will give us what we ask for in accordance with His will. God may say no if that is what's best for us, but He will never say yes if we don't ask Him.

When it came to my desire to have a significant other in high school, I can see now that I was very selfish about it. It was all about me being happy and not about me finding someone who would encourage me to stay connected to God. I can remember praying for that special someone very often during my early college years. God did not answer my prayers as soon as I would have liked Him to at the time, but I can see now how He waited until I was seeking someone who would draw me closer to Him. Despite how you may feel, God is there, and He does hear you. So, the next time you have a deep desire for something, take your request to God. He may not always answer the way you want Him to, but I know He will do what is best for you.

Prayer

Dear Father, please help me to come to You when I have desires on my heart. I ask that You guide me to seek things that pull me closer to You. Amen.

Personal Reflection

Think of something that you really want. Have you prayed for this thing? Also, reflect on this desire, and ask yourself if this will draw you closer to God.

Want To Be A Cool Kid?

17 Do not let your heart envy sinners,
but always be zealous for the fear of the Lord.

-Proverbs 23:17

D ID YOU WANT to be one of the cool kids in school? Do you know that feeling of wanting to be the life of the party or to be the most attractive person at work? Personally, I can relate with anyone who has thought any of these thoughts. I was far from one of the cool kids at school and don't think that I was ever invited to a party. I got turned down by more girls in high school than I can even remember. To top it off, I was always the guy at work who didn't swear, which made me stand out in several situations. I tried to be content with who I was, but that didn't stop me from having some desires to be like the guys that all of the girls wanted to go out with. There were times it would have seemed nice to "have it all." However, I can see now more than ever how it was a blessing that I was not one of those kids. It is not always easy to see why God puts us in the position that He does, but it is important to remember there is always a reason. Today's devotion is all about how our envious and jealous desires may take our focus away from what is truly important.

If you think about it, being popular is not a bad thing, right? I mean, if you have the ability to be the best basketball player in the world, then that is awesome! But, is it possible that the environment that surrounds our desires could impact our relationship with God? When we commit ourselves to something of this world, are we aware of the snares and traps that surround that desire? This is something that is not fun to think about because it happens to all of us. If you and I truly evaluate ourselves, we have all wanted to be that "cool person" at one point in our lives. Maybe you have wanted to be that person who sounded cool when they swore or talked about how they were sought after by the opposite sex. While there are times we get caught up in wanting to be someone else, never fail to see how God can use situations to help you see the beauty in who you are.

As Christians, we know how amazing God is and how great He is to us. He loves us so much that He sacrificed His own Son to pay for our sins so we could inherit the gift of eternal life in Heaven. There are a lot of cool things in this world, but none of them come even close to matching the awesome blessings God has in store for us! Personally, there are times in my past that it felt like being the lady's man or the guy doing the keg stand would have been awesome. But trust me, nothing compares to being the guy whose heart is after Jesus.

Prayer

Dear Lord, please help me to seek You above all else. I am often tempted to act in a way that is cool in the eyes of the world, but not in Yours. Please guide my heart to serve You in all that I do despite how people might look at me. In Your name I pray. Amen.

Personal Reflection

Think of one time in your life when you wanted to be something that you are not. Would that change in your life have brought you closer to God, or would it have drawn you away from Him? Based on what you know about yourself, how can you better seek God instead of the ways of the world in the future?

Day 4

Beware of Your Surroundings

[16] For where you have envy and selfish ambition, there you find disorder and every evil practice.

-James 3:16

H OW DO YOU feel about the world around you? Is it comfortable and loving, or is there a lot of stress and anger? Do you feel closer to God when you step out your front door every day, or farther away? Is there peace or tension? I am asking some pretty deep questions here but for good reason. There is no denying that we all live in a sinful world full of problems, but we can control how we embrace the world around us. How we think, speak, and act all plays a role in how we impact our homes, communities, and the world as a whole. As we dig deeper into the topic of envy today, I really want to encourage you to evaluate how you impact the world around you.

The verse above from James is one that can seem really scary on the surface. To read and to know that every evil practice of this world can be found where envy and selfish ambitions exist is unsettling. However, is it possible that the words above can be taken as encouragement? That may not be the feeling you have right now, but let me explain. If we are in a place where envy runs rampant and controls the environment, are we not possibly part of the problem? If your kids or younger siblings are never content and always want more, is it possible they think that way because others (possibly you) in their lives think the same way? I'm not making any accusations here, but I just want us to be honest about the role we play in the world around us.

We are all sinful and make mistakes, but we cannot let a poor attitude deter us from serving God and His Kingdom. Our Lord is there to help us when we fall. He is there to encourage us through His Word and through fellow Christians. It may seem impossible to show contentment and selflessness in our thoughts, words, and actions, but it can be done!

When it comes down to the *why* behind our need to be content, James 3:16 lays this concept out perfectly. When we are selfish and envy what others have, we not only do damage to our own hearts, but we contribute to the disorder that takes place around us every day. Staying connected to God is crucially important when we are struggling to give thanks for all the blessings we already have. Never forget that you are not in this alone. You will always have God by your side and many times may have fellow Christians to encourage you as you strive to be a positive light in this world.

Prayer

Dear Father in Heaven, please help me to be content with what I have. My life often gets so congested by the idea that I need more when I really don't. I ask that You help me to feel full and satisfied through faith in You. Amen.

Personal Reflection

How would you evaluate your lifestyle in light of our verse from today? Is your personal attitude one that is content or one that always wants more? What can you do to be a positive light of contentment and selflessness in the environment around you?

Day 5

Give Thanks!

¹ Shout for joy to the Lord, all the earth.² Worship the Lord with gladness; come before him with joyful songs. ³ Know that the Lord is God. It is he who made us, and we are his; we are his people, the sheep of his pasture. ⁴ Enter his gates with thanksgiving and his courts with praise; give thanks to him and praise his name. ⁵ For the Lord is good and his love endures forever; his faithfulness continues through all generations.

-Psalm 100

D O YOU EVER sit back and think about how richly God has blessed you? Do you take time to give Him praise because of how great He is? Despite every struggle that I have faced in this life, there is no doubt God has blessed me richly. He has given me my family and friends along with my gifts and abilities. I know God is truly the source of it all, but I'll openly admit to you that He does not always get the thanks and praise He deserves. The truth is that everyone falls short of giving God the credit He deserves. Despite where you or I are at with giving God thanks and praise, we can both admit that we could do better. Today's devotion is all about not letting our envious thoughts get in the way of giving gratitude to the One who deserves it most.

As you look at the words above from Psalm 100, it is hard not to feel a rush of encouragement and joy! For the first time in this chapter, we are digging into the flip side of the struggles with envy that we face. Thanking and praising God for all of His goodness in our lives is very important. He is the giver of all that has been, is now, and will ever be. He gave us life through the gift of the Holy Spirit and lives in us every day. When it comes down to it, we have so much more than we could ever ask for. Eternal life in Heaven is ours through faith in Jesus! Does it get any better than that?

To close this devotion, I want to take you back to my childhood. Whenever my brother or I would get a present or a card for a birthday or holiday, my mom was always extremely forward about the importance of saying thank you. Whether it was in person or in a thank you card, she always put a large amount of value on the meaning of those two words. As you work through the rest of this book and move on to a new one, my hope is that you never stop thanking God for all the blessings He has given you.

Prayer

Dear God, thank You for every last blessing You have given me. Amen.

Personal Reflection

Think of something that God has blessed you with recently. This can be something big or small. Have you thanked God for that blessing? If not, how can you do a better job of making sure to thank God for your blessings in the future?

Day 6

True Love

⁴ Love is patient, love is kind. It does not envy, it does not boast, it is not proud. ⁵ It does not dishonor others, it is not self-seeking, it is not easily angered, it keeps no record of wrongs. ⁶ Love does not delight in evil but rejoices with the truth. ⁷ It always protects, always trusts, always hopes, always perseveres.

-1 Corinthians 13:4-7

H OW DOES ENVY affect the relationships you have with others? Personally, I would say this chain does not play a big role in any of my relationships, but I would be lying if I said it didn't at all. For those of you who have been engaged and understand the process of preparing for marriage, you may be able to relate to the current stage of my life. As the days count down to my wedding day, it is becoming more and more evident how important it is for me to encourage and celebrate Sarah's successes. It's not that I haven't to this point, but it is becoming very clear to me that being completely selfless in every element of love is even more important than I could have perceived in my younger years. As we dig into these verses from 1 Corinthians, I really want to encourage you to evaluate every element of what love is and what it is not.

As you read the verses above, it becomes pretty clear that there are a lot of things that love is and many other things that it is not. Verse four states that love does not envy, but I want to encourage you to dig deeper into this passage and place envy alongside every adjective that love is. Is there any place for envy within anything that love is?

To close, I want to be transparent with you about some of the envy in my life. Sarah and I are both blessed with the opportunity to work a full-time career in the field we graduated in. However, there is a difference in the amount of money we make that sometimes leads my heart to envy. She makes more than I do, which is a great thing, but there is still that little piece of me that is jealous and wants to be making more so I can be the breadwinner when we are married. This struggle, while small and seemingly isolated, has led me to be less loving in other areas of our relationship. I'm not telling you this to vent but to let you know you are not alone if you face the same struggle. The chain of envy has the ability to affect how we love others in many ways. May God be with us as we strive to be examples of what love is in a world that sees so much of what love is not.

Prayer

Dear Lord, please guide my heart to see how richly You have blessed me. The presence of Your love is truly amazing, and I ask that You help me to never take it for granted. Please lead me with Your Spirit to love more and to envy less. Amen.

Personal Reflection

Think of someone in your life who you envy with a heavy heart. Maybe this person has a nicer home, car, etc. How has your jealousy affected your love for that person? Say a prayer, and ask God to help you suppress this envy so that you can more effectively show this person love going forward.

Day 7

The Simple Basics

16 Rejoice always, 17 pray continually, 18 give thanks in all circumstances; for this is God's will for you in Christ Jesus.
                                                        -1 Thessalonians 5:16-18

T HIS CHAPTER HAS been all about a chain that can add extra weight to countless struggles. It can be easy to let envy drag us down and defeat us. As we have learned with every chain before this one, it is critically important to remember we are not alone! God is with us and will help us battle any struggle that we are facing. Everything up to this point in the chapter has been about uncovering what envy is. Today is all about going into combat and battling with this struggle while knowing we have an amazing God by our side.

As we dig into the Scripture reading from today, I want to break this section down and evaluate it verse by verse. All three of these verses are very straightforward, but there is more to them than you might think. For instance, verse 16 reminds us to "rejoice always." That may sound as simple as "be happy all the time," but this piece of encouragement from the apostle Paul goes so much deeper. To the world, rejoicing always would not make sense, but Christians have a reason to be joyful every day. We get to live in light of the amazing fact that Jesus died for our sins and that the gift of eternal life is ours through faith in Him. A Christian's joy is not based on circumstance but is something that is ever-present through faith.

Verse 17 states very simply to "pray continually." As Christians, we know that deep struggles with sin call for prayer. The Bible verses that are found in this chapter are evidence of how destructive envy can be in our lives. My encouragement for you is to pray often about envy regardless of how much or little you struggle with it. Closeness with God reveals to us how His presence can help us break any chain in our lives.

Verse 18 may be the toughest element of this piece to get a solid grasp on. "Give thanks in ALL circumstances." This means we should give thanks when we are struggling to pay the bills while our neighbor just bought a new car. All circumstances even include those times when we are put down for our faith. There is nothing about this concept that is easy, but we can be encouraged through faith to know it is possible. We may fall short in how often we rejoice or pray or give thanks, but don't lose hope. God is there for us and will help us to fight through every struggle this life throws at us. We can't break the chain of envy alone, but we can be assured through the presence of the Holy Spirit that God will help us to rejoice, pray, and give thanks more and more every day.

Prayer

Dear Father, thank You for such wonderful guiding words like the ones found in the Scripture reading from today. Please help me to pray in the midst of every struggle, including envy. Thank You for always being there for me. Amen.

Personal Reflection

Over the course of the next week, establish some extra time to say a prayer about the struggles that you are currently dealing with including envy.

7

Anger

Day 1

Don't Go To Bed Angry

26 "In your anger do not sin": Do not let the sun go down while you are still angry, 27 and do not give the devil a foothold.

-Ephesians 4:26-27

H AVE YOU EVER heard the phrase, "don't go to bed angry"? In most cases I have heard this said to or about married couples. Within a marriage, it is good to leave all of the anger from the day behind and to start fresh the next day. Despite the fact that this phrase is more common when talking about marriage, it applies to all of us. Anger is something that can affect everyone and therefore needs to be addressed for what it is. Anger is not always a sin, but this element of our lives becomes a chain when Satan uses it to get the best of us.

As we look at the words above that the apostle Paul was inspired to write, it is very clear that God is opposed to His people carrying anger with them. Again, it is not necessarily a sin to be angry, but verse 27 sheds a very clear light on what can happen when we let our anger hang around. Anger is like a ticking time bomb. For some of us, the bomb goes off after a few ticks. For others, it may take months or even years for their anger to build up in a way that produces an explosion. If we don't defuse the bomb every night, we increase the chances of allowing an explosion to happen. Explosions of anger can lead to a multitude of sins, and that is why this chain in our lives needs to be addressed. We need to know as Christians that anger can be very dangerous and should not be taken lightly.

Now that we have addressed the bomb in the room and know that it needs to be defused, let's take some time and address how we can do that. When your day comes to an end, there may be a little or a lot of anger on your heart. Regardless of your situation, it is important to get the bomb out in clear sight so it can be taken care of. The world offers many methods to deal with anger that may or may not work. As Christians, we can be assured that there is always one method that does work, which is prayer. Talking to God about your anger and asking Him for relief is a surefire strategy to defuse all of the bombs you accumulated over the course of a day. If you are someone who struggles with anger on a deep level, it may be good to call upon some resources that God has placed in your life to help you better defuse your anger. Despite the strong or weak effects that this chain has on you, I want to encourage you to ask God to give you strength in this battle.

Prayer

Dear Jesus, please help me to defuse all of my anger from the day before I go to sleep tonight. I know Satan uses my anger to cause explosions of sin. Guide my heart to be calm and collected in a way that honors You. Amen.

Personal Reflection

What makes you angry? Is this source of anger something that you have carried with you? If so, how can you better defuse your anger within the day so it does not carry on to the next day?

Day 2

Simple, but Tough Implications

¹⁹ My dear brothers and sisters, take note of this: Everyone should be quick to listen, slow to speak and slow to become angry, ²⁰ because human anger does not produce the righteousness that God desires.

-James 1:19-20

WERE YOU EVER told as a child to think before you speak? Between my parents and my teachers, "think before you speak" was a very common phrase in my life. It seems so simple, doesn't it? As a young child, I knew this phrase was important, but I don't know if I really understood why until I got older. It is always good to think before you speak. However, there may be an argument to say that this phrase is even more important when addressing anger. As we dig into these verses from James, I really want to encourage you to keep "think before you speak" on your heart and mind.

When looking at the verses above, there may be one element that does not match up with what we have been talking about in this chapter. We have already discussed how all anger is not bad anger. Verse 20 says: "human anger does not produce the righteousness that God desires." This may not look right at first, but it is true. *Human* anger, which could be also stated as "anger of the human flesh" or "sinful anger" is not good or healthy. The only good kind of anger is righteous anger, which only comes through faith.

Now that we have a definition of the anger being talked about in this verse, let's take a look back at verse 19 and break it into three pieces:

1. Quick to listen
2. Slow to speak
3. Slow to become angry

One of the things that I love about the Bible is that it is often very straightforward. These verses state that there is one thing we should do quickly and two we should do slowly. It is very simple, but you and I both know that following this is far from easy. As you continue through the rest of this chapter on anger, I want to encourage you to use these three basic ideas and apply them to your daily life. Even if you are the mildest person in the world, there is a place in your life for these verses from James 1. Also, never forget you are not alone. God is there and will help you to love Him better in how you embrace these verses. Our Father in Heaven is quick to listen, slow to speak, and slow to become angry.

Prayer
Dear God, please help me to show You love by being quick to listen, slow to speak, and slow to become angry. Amen.

Personal Reflection
Is the principle of "think before you speak" something that you apply in your daily life? Regardless of how much or little you use it, think of ways you can better love God by doing this in the week ahead.

Day 3

The Depths of the Law

[21] *"You have heard that it was said to the people long ago, 'You shall not murder, and anyone who murders will be subject to judgment.' [22] But I tell you that anyone who is angry with a brother or sister will be subject to judgment.*

-Matthew 5:21-22a

WHAT DO YOU think of when you hear the word "murder"? Within the culture of the United States, this term stands for a crime that is probably considered to be the worst of crimes. If someone is on trial for murder, anyone and everyone knows the punishment is very steep if convicted. Murderers are often sentenced to life in prison and sometimes even face the death penalty. It only makes sense that a terrible crime such as taking a life should be met with harsh consequences. That being said, are there times as Christians that we overemphasis the sins the world deems as terrible to cover up our own wrongs?

Upon looking at these verses from Matthew, it almost seems hard to believe that Jesus would make this comparison. As humans who are used to the legal standards of our national culture, it can be really hard to grasp the point our Savior is making here. Before we go any further, I want you to mentally step outside of your earthly understanding of the law to focus on the concept Jesus is laying out for us. Now, as we look at verse 21, we see a statement that tracks with humankind very well. Anyone who murders will be subject to judgement. That makes sense, however, does verse 22 grab our attention in the same way? It almost seems like Jesus is putting the sin of murder and human anger on the same level. Believe it or not, that is exactly what Jesus is doing, and He is making a great point. When it comes to sin, God does not have a grid that shows which sins are less or more punishable. The reality of sin and the Law is that all sins are punishable by eternal death. Thankfully, Jesus suffered death and rose from the grave so that our sins would be washed away. We have no need to worry, but we do need to be real about how our human anger hurts our neighbor. Our God asks us to love Him and one another, and human anger does not show others love but does the opposite. The bottom line is that our human anger is a sin, and we need to be honest with ourselves about that. Once we acknowledge our sinful anger, we can approach God with confidence and ask Him to help us battle this struggle in our lives.

Anger is something that may seem harmless in comparison to things like murder. However, never let the minimization of this issue pull you away from the truth that Jesus displays for us here in Matthew. We all get angry. Some more than others, but regardless, we all need forgiveness and strength that only God can provide. Never forget that God is there to strengthen you and to help you break chains in your life, such as anger.

Prayer

Dear Lord, please help me to avoid sinful anger. I know it leads to nothing good and only pulls me away from You. Please guide me to love You and others better every day. Amen.

Personal Reflection

How do you feel when you read these words from Matthew 5? Do they inspire you? Do they frustrate you? How can you better embrace these words in your life going forward?

Day 4

Beware the Path

1 Do not fret because of those who are evil
or be envious of those who do wrong;
7 Be still before the Lord and wait patiently for him;
do not fret when people succeed in their ways,
when they carry out their wicked schemes.
8 Refrain from anger and turn from wrath; do not fret—it leads
only to evil.

-Psalm 37:1, 7-8

I WANT YOU TO take a mental walk back to your childhood and think of a time when you did something wrong? Maybe you saw something on TV or at school that seemed really cool, so you thought you would give it a try. Maybe you said a swear word or a vulgar phrase that sounded cool when you first heard it. Now, I want you to fast-forward to when you got caught doing that bad or wrong thing. If you were anything like I was as a kid, you might have gotten a little frustrated and angry when you got caught because you wanted to keep doing that "cool" thing. Today's devotion is about how we can address the anger that comes from wanting things that hurt our relationships with God.

The verses above from Psalm 37 draw a basic picture of right and wrong. It may seem a little juvenile to address basics like these, but they are very important. These words from Psalms outline what anger that comes from envying sinful behavior produces: evil. That is a very deep and cutting word, but it is true. Anger that comes from desiring what others gain through rejecting God is evil.

On the surface, it can seem very exhilarating to do things that oppose God. Saying something that hurts God but has a nice ring to it can often give us a feeling of temporary satisfaction. That being said, we know there is a much greater life beyond this one. We all get a time of grace to live on this earth. Over the course of the decades we live here, it can be easy to get caught up in all of the temporary things that give us thrills. However, we must never forget the gift of eternal life that is ours. Jesus shed His blood on the cross so we could live with Him in prosperity for all of eternity. We may get frustrated and angry at times when we feel left out of the fun that is here on Earth, but never forget that the narrow path we are on is the one that leads to the gift of eternal paradise.

Prayer

Dear Jesus, thank You for dying on the cross to save me from my sins. Please guide me to live for You every day. Help me not to get angry when I lack what others have but to give thanks for all the blessings You have showered upon me. Amen.

Personal Reflection

Think of a time when you wanted something that led to sinful behavior. Why did this appeal to you, and how can you better focus your eyes on Jesus in the future?

Day 5

Protect Your Walls

32 Whoever is slow to anger is better than the mighty,
and he who rules his spirit than he who takes a city.

-Proverbs 16:32, ESV

28 A man without self-control
is like a city broken into and left without walls.

-Proverbs 25:28, ESV

H OW ARE THE walls of your life doing? Are they really strong with iron bars running through them, or are they weak and ready to crumble when the next breeze comes? Do they have a good support force, or is one person (you) trying to keep them standing up? Anger is something that can really get the best of us if we don't have it together. Self-control is something Christians strive to practice in their daily lives, but sadly those walls break down on us all from time to time. We have already touched on how we can defuse our anger in a Godly way. Now it is time to dig into how we can suppress or captivate that anger in times when it is not appropriate or good to get it out.

The proverbs above are composed of words that God inspired King Solomon to write about the importance of self-control. These passages reference a military mindset that displays the relationship of anger and self-control. In this time period, it was very common for cities to build walls around their borders to protect them from their enemies. If the walls of a nation were torn down, this would leave them completely exposed and most likely defeated. The same concept goes for us when it comes to anger. If we allow our walls to get weak and feeble, then it is likely our anger will explode, which will leave us susceptible to attacks from the devil. This may sound like a really scary element of our lives, but we know through faith that we don't have to shore up our walls alone. God is there for us and will help us to build our walls of self-control if we ask Him. We should also never forget that we have the gift of the Holy Spirit living in us every single day. Maintaining our "city" is not all on us. We have the greatest support force in the world. We are never alone when our walls of self-control start breaking down.

Prayer

Dear Father, there are too many times when my walls get weak and my anger flies. Help me to be self-controlled and to honor You in all that I do. Amen.

Personal Reflection

Over the course of a regular week, think of common situations that may cause your walls of self-control to become weak. How do these situations arise? Do your actions play a role in your rising anger, and how can you better prepare for situations where your walls of self-control are under fire?

Day 6

Endure with the Lord's Help

13 One day when Job's sons and daughters were feasting and drinking wine at the oldest brother's house, 14 a messenger came to Job and said, "The oxen were plowing and the donkeys were grazing nearby, 15 and the Sabeans attacked and made off with them. They put the servants to the sword, and I am the only one who has escaped to tell you!"16 While he was still speaking, another messenger came and said, "The fire of God fell from the heavens and burned up the sheep and the servants, and I am the only one who has escaped to tell you!" 17 While he was still speaking, another messenger came and said, "The Chaldeans formed three raiding parties and swept down on your camels and made off with them. They put the servants to the sword, and I am the only one who has escaped to tell you!" 18 While he was still speaking, yet another messenger came and said, "Your sons and daughters were feasting and drinking wine at the oldest brother's house, 19 when suddenly a mighty wind swept in from the desert and struck the four corners of the house. It collapsed on them and they are dead, and I am the only one who has escaped to tell you!" 20 At this, Job got up and tore his robe and shaved his head. Then he fell to the ground in worship 21 and said: "Naked I came from my mother's womb, and naked I will depart. The Lord gave and the Lord has taken away; may the name of the Lord be praised." 22 In all this, Job did not sin by charging God with wrongdoing.

-Job 1:13-22

W HEN YOU LOOK at these verses, do you wonder how Job didn't lose his cool? As someone who struggles with the thought of loved ones going through pain or dying, I cannot even grasp the gravity of this situation. Job's family and all of his belongings were taken away from him. By most standards, he had nothing left. Nothing! In a situation like this, it would seem understandable for Job to be upset to the point of screaming in anger at God. But, as these verses show, Job did the exact opposite. After losing just about everything that meant anything to him on this earth, he fell to the ground and worshiped God. He didn't ask God why and didn't question the situation. He worshiped Him. As we consider the anger that is on our hearts, I would encourage you to think of Job when things get tough. It may be very hard to keep it together in times when life doesn't go our way, but always remember that God is there for us. My hope is that this example from Job will encourage you to turn from anger and to worship God even when things get tough.

Prayer

Dear God, please help me to be more like Job. I often get angry when You don't give me what I want. Please guide my heart to worship You in good times and in bad. Amen.

Personal Reflection

How can you be more like Job?

Day 7

Lead with Peace

15 A gentle answer turns away wrath, but a harsh word stirs up anger

-Proverbs 15:1

A S WE FINISH this chapter on anger, my hope is that you are feeling encouraged and inspired. When it comes to talking about the elements of our earthly lives that pull us away from God, it can be easy to feel like there is a finger pointing right at our souls. My personal opinion is that many Christians have gotten really good at pointing the finger instead of loving each other. Today's devotion is all about encouraging you to seek God and His desire for your life as you read through the rest of this book. The sad reality for every one of us is that our human anger drags us down and causes us to sin against God and others. As we study this last piece of Scripture on anger, I hope your heart is moved in a way that inspires you to love God and others more today than you did the day before.

The proverb above is very simple but does a great job of reminding us of how impactful our words are. In the 21st century, posting on social media is perhaps the most popular means of venting anger. Unlike decades or centuries ago, we now have a place where we can openly vent our anger without any concern about how those words will affect others. We don't see the celebrities who are constantly dealing with the harsh words or the teenaged girl who is crying in her bedroom because the whole school learned about the most embarrassing thing in her life on social media that other girls posted out of spite. We don't see the heart of the politician who is trying to do the right thing but is burdened by the thousands of angry posts and letters they receive every day. We don't see the results of our anger and often hide behind our computer screens instead of facing what we have done. We have almost become immune to dealing with the anger that is stirring in our world every day. It is time to separate ourselves from the constant stream of anger. As Christians, we know through the love of Jesus that we have a greater calling. We might not be able to stop the constant turmoil that is taking place in our world, but we can be a source of peace and encouragement that makes others question their anger. God enables us through the gift of His Spirit to be a light in a dark world. To be a gentle answer in a place where harsh words are the norm. We may be looked at as counter-cultural, but who cares? We have Jesus on our side, and nothing beats that!

Prayer

Dear Holy Spirit, please lead my heart to speak with kind and gentle words. The last thing I want to do is hurt others when I get angry. Yet, I struggle and know I need Your help. Please guide me to be a light for Christ in how I act, speak, post, and think. In the name of Jesus I pray. Amen.

Personal Reflection

Can you think of a time when you vented your anger on social media? Maybe you were upset at someone. Maybe your team lost and you wanted to let the world know that you thought the coach needed to be fired. Whatever the case was, take this instance of anger and think of ways you could have been kind and gentle in this situation. How can you do a better job of being a light for Christ in the future?

8

Money

Day 1

Reality at Its Roots

10 For the love of money is a root of all kinds of evil. Some people, eager for money, have wandered from the faith and pierced themselves with many griefs.

-1 Timothy 6:10

D O YOU HAVE any rich friends? Are there people in your life who have wealth to the degree where it appears they can't even spend their money? To follow up these questions, I want to ask you a few more. Do you have friends or family members who have a deep desire to be rich? Maybe you are close with some people who want to live in nice mansions and drive luxurious cars? Are you one of these people? If you look around, you can probably find someone in your life, possibly including yourself, who wants to be rich. This chapter is all about how money and wealth can be a heavy chain in our lives of faith. Before we go any deeper, understand there is nothing wrong with being rich. The questions above can be used as tools to differentiate wealth from the desire for wealth because it is the desire that unfortunately leads many hearts away from God.

As we look at the verse above from 1 Timothy, it is evident that loving money can have some very serious implications. Having a deep hunger for wealth is not a surface issue, but rather defines itself as the root system of all kinds of evil. As this verse goes on to say "eagerness for money has led many away from the faith." All of the chains we have studied have that potential, but it may be fair to say that a desire for money has led more people away from God than other chains. Only God knows the facts on this issue, but living in the United States draws a pretty clear picture of how wealth and prosperity can gradually draw people away from Him.

So, is this chain of money something that is weighing on your heart?

I think all of us can say it does at times, but I don't want those of you who are content to write this chain off as something less important. A hunger for wealth has the potential to grow slowly, but also consistently. Think of your desire for money as a thistle. When small, a thistle is a little pokey but has a weak root system, so it is easy to pull out. If we don't keep our eyes on this thistle of desire in our lives, it will grow to a point where it will be extremely hard, and not to mention painful to pull out. As you work through the rest of this chapter, my hope is that you will embrace God's Word and call upon Him when you are deep in the weeds. He is always there for you and will guide your heart in the right direction if you ask Him.

Prayer

Dear Father in Heaven, please guide my heart to be content with the money I have. I know I don't need more, but it is so hard to be content when others have more than me. Please help me to invest my whole heart into loving You. Amen.

Personal Reflection

Is money a chain you have struggled with over the course of your lifetime? If so, how has this chain distanced you from God? If you are a content person, how can you ask God to help you resist the temptation of desiring worldly wealth?

Day 2

Loveless Love

10 Whoever loves money never has enough; whoever loves wealth is never satisfied with their income. This too is meaningless.

-Ecclesiastes 5:10

I WANT YOU TO think back to a time during your childhood or teenaged years when you were growing. Personally, I can remember how excited I was to grow another inch taller. My biggest growth spurt came when I grew nine inches over the course of 18 months in middle school. I loved growing taller and being tall, but there was one part of growing that was a little annoying. I was never full! I mean, never. I could eat from the time I woke up in the morning until the time I went to bed and never be full. I want you to encompass that feeling of never being full. Then, apply this frame of mind to the topic of this chapter and carry it with you today. We know that loving money is a desire with deep roots, but we may often forget where our hunger for wealth leads.

As you look at the verse above, I want to introduce you to the author of this book. It is believed that King Solomon wrote the book of Ecclesiastes. For those of you who don't know about this guy, he has a unique background. At the beginning of 2 Chronicles, God offered to give King Solomon anything he wanted. Anything! Solomon could have asked for an endless amount of money. He could have asked for relationships or strength over other nations, but he didn't. He asked for wisdom. The words above were inspired by God and were written by a man who already had great wealth. Solomon knew that no amount of wealth would make him happier. He knew where fullness could be found and understood that the riches of the world were meaningless in the grand scheme of things. God could have inspired anyone to write these words, but He chose someone who had wealth and made a point in doing so. It doesn't matter how much or how little you have. It does not matter if your house is big or small or, if your car is new or old. It doesn't matter if you are a wealthy king or a waiter making minimum wage. All that truly matters in this world is your faith in God.

As you continue through your day and through the rest of this chapter, I don't want you to go hungry. I don't want you to be starving for something that will never fill you up. Rather, my hope is that you will seek the only one who can make you full. Whether you see it right now or not, your faith is the most valuable and fulfilling thing you have in your life. Rather than seeking an endless chain of hunger, may God lead you to seek a path that leads to an eternal life of fullness with Him.

Prayer

Dear God, please fill me up with Your love, and surround me with Your presence. I know that loving money will only lead down a road of starvation. Please help me to stay on the path that leads to eternal life in Heaven with You. Amen.

Personal Reflection

Have you ever been on a path in life that has always left you hungry for more? Reflect on that journey and ask yourself: how could I better embrace the fullness that is found through faith?

Day 3

Possessions Fail

¹⁹ "Do not store up for yourselves treasures on earth, where moths and vermin destroy, and where thieves break in and steal. ²⁰ But store up for yourselves treasures in heaven, where moths and vermin do not destroy, and where thieves do not break in and steal. ²¹ For where your treasure is, there your heart will be also.

-Matthew 6:19-21

ARE YOU A saver or a spender? Personally, I am a big-time saver. I am always looking to put money away before I look to spend it on something. This is an attitude and way of life that has run in my family for generations. That being said, you may be a spender. When you get a paycheck, it may mean way more to you to live in the moment rather than saving for later. There is nothing wrong with being a saver or a spender, but where our heart is within our actions does matter. As we work through this devotion today, I want to ask you to reflect on this question: what is your greatest treasure?

How do you react when you read the verses above from Matthew? Regardless of being a saver or a spender, there is a good chance that Jesus' words hit you in the heart. This world teaches us to accumulate as much wealth as we can in order to live life to the fullest. While there is nothing wrong with making the best of the time of grace we are given here on Earth, Jesus does lay things out pretty bluntly. If our goal is to treasure this earth and what it offers, then there is a guarantee that we will be left empty. There is nothing in this world that will provide treasure with the likes of what Jesus offers. Eternal life in Heaven is not just something that is good or great. It is amazing! Nothing will ever be able to compare to a place without pain and sadness. Heaven is perfect in every way, and this treasure is ours, not because we have earned or deserved it, but because Jesus paid the price so we could enjoy His gift to us.

Whether you are a saver or a spender, there are temptations you will face when it comes to money. Some of us will be tempted to save every dime we can until we die, as if we are taking it with us. Others will struggle with the idea of leaving the parties and experiences of this earth behind. Regardless of who you are and how you are tempted, never forget where your greatest treasure lies. It may be really tough to keep your focus on God, but never forget that the Holy Spirit is there to help you focus on what is really important.

Prayer

Dear Jesus, thank You for dying on the cross so that I could have the treasure of eternal life with You! Please guide me to seek You over all of the treasures this world holds. Amen.

Personal Reflection

What earthly treasures do you hold close to your heart? Now, think of how you observe these blessings. Are they viewed as gifts from God, or do they pull your heart closer to the world and farther from God? Think of ways you can view your possessions as gifts and blessings rather than allowing them to become hindrances.

Day 4

Seek the Provider

^{27} "Consider how the wild flowers grow. They do not labor or spin. Yet I tell you, not even Solomon in all his splendor was dressed like one of these. ^{28} If that is how God clothes the grass of the field, which is here today, and tomorrow is thrown into the fire, how much more will he clothe you—you of little faith! ^{29} And do not set your heart on what you will eat or drink; do not worry about it. ^{30} For the pagan world runs after all such things, and your Father knows that you need them. ^{31} But seek his kingdom, and these things will be given to you as well.

-Luke 12:27-31

HAVE YOU EVER been tempted to think that God didn't know or understand you needs? That He didn't get you were going through a tough time and needed Him to come through for you? As Christians, thoughts like these can cross our minds in many different forms. For instance, when we struggle financially or have a hard time just keeping food on the table, it can be hard to see and understand why God isn't stepping in. Questions like: *why isn't He blessing me with a good job so I can earn a better income?* may cross your mind. We all live in a world full of sin. A world that is full of crying, grief, and pain. All that being said, we also have the privilege of living in light of the fact that God is with us every day. Today's devotion is really going to zero in on our needs and how God provides.

The verses above from Luke 12 display some very simple language that can be very hard to understand in tough times. When things get rough and this sinful world gets to us, we may often worry when God does not resolve things how we would like Him to. It can be easy to question what God is doing and why He is doing things in a certain way. When the worrying gets worse, we may even push God away and try to take things into our own hands. While handling things on our own and seeking a source of income with no regard for God may seem plausible, these words from Jesus tell us a different story. The truth is that our Father in Heaven will always provide us with what we need. In God's eyes, our needs may not include a high-paying job or designer clothing, but He knows our needs. In fact, He knows them better than we do.

In this life, the odds are good that you will be tempted to think that God is not there for you every now and then. The world wants us to think God has abandoned us when things get tough, but don't be deceived. Our Father in Heaven will always be there to provide for us. There is no need to push Him out, and my encouragement for you is to be patient. Every day is a blessing from God, and when it comes to money or anything for that matter, He will always provide everything we need.

Prayer

Lord, please help me to be content with what I have. I am often tempted to think that I don't have enough, and then I try to take things into my own hands. I know that everything I have is a gift from You and ask You to help me to live this life in a way that says thank You for every last blessing. Amen.

Personal Reflection

Think of a time when if felt like God wasn't there. When it seemed like there was no other option than to take things into your own hands. How can you better embrace God's presence and believe in His ability to provide going forward?

Day 5

The Value of a True Heart

⁴¹ Jesus sat down opposite the place where the offerings were put and watched the crowd putting their money into the temple treasury. Many rich people threw in large amounts. ⁴² But a poor widow came and put in two very small copper coins, worth only a few cents. ⁴³ Calling his disciples to him, Jesus said, "Truly I tell you, this poor widow has put more into the treasury than all the others. ⁴⁴ They all gave out of their wealth; but she, out of her poverty, put in everything—all she had to live on."

-Mark 12:41-44

WHAT FEELINGS AND emotions go through your mind when you realize your pastor or priest is starting the "money sermon"? For a lot of churches, this topic comes up one Sunday a year. If your church does sermon series, you might get a few weeks on this topic at the most. Beyond that, money does not get a lot of air time. I can tell you there are not many pastors who enjoy the money sermon. It's not a fun topic, right? Much of the time, money matters within the church is a sensitive topic. We don't like to talk about it, but we need to. When roots of desiring wealth grow deep, it can be really easy to forget about giving back to God or just giving in general.

The verses above are perhaps some of the most touching verses in the Bible. I can picture being there with Jesus by the temple treasury watching this all take place. Can you imagine watching the wealthy giving their large amounts of money, and then seeing this woman put everything she had into the offering plate. To put this into today's standards, imagine watching millionaires dropping checks for $1,000 into the offering plate, then seeing a homeless man give his last dollar. Those thousands mean nothing to a wealthy man, but that $1 would only be enough to buy the poor man food for the day. This image is very powerful and really guides our hearts to reflect on the question: where is my heart really at?

As you reflect on the financial means that God has blessed you with, my hope is that you are dedicated to giving back to God in a full manner. It can be hard to know or understand how much to put in the offering plate, but don't get frustrated. Rather, just be honest and genuinely search your heart for the answer. If finding this answer is a struggle for you, pray about it. Ask God to guide you to see how you can give fully. Remember, our Savior is not after your money. He is after your heart.

Prayer

Dear Holy Spirit, please lead me to give with a true heart. I want to give with everything that I have, but I am struggling. Please assure me of Your presence and guide me to be more like that poor widow. Amen.

Personal Reflection

As you go through the rest of your day and week, reflect on the heart of the poor widow and think of ways that you could be more like her.

Day 6

Embrace Spiritual Wealth

⁵ Keep your lives free from the love of money and be content with what you have, because God has said, "Never will I leave you; never will I forsake you."

-Hebrews 13:5

D O YOU FEEL wealthy? Do you feel like you have it all? For me, I definitely feel blessed in many ways, but I can't say that I think of myself as financially wealthy. I graduated college less than a month ago, so I have a pretty good amount of student debt to pay off. Also, I am just starting out in my career, so my financial means look small compared to co-workers and friends. Even though I am no longer a broke college kid, it is still easy to feel like one. This devotion is not about wealth that you or I can see. It is about the wealth we have through faith, which is so much greater than we often give it credit for.

How many times each day do you sit back and embrace the amazingness that is God's presence? Personally, I can't say that I do this enough. The reality of our lives is that God is always there for us. He will never leave us, forsake us, or stop loving us. Yet, do we take the time to give thanks for that? All too often, we can probably say that we doubt His presence and cling to the world rather than reaching out to Him. We know through faith that this is a really counterintuitive way to carry out our lives, but yet we still do it. We use our money as a backup when it doesn't feel like God is there. We may even steal or hurt others to gain things that we think we need when we really don't. If there is anything that we have learned by this point in the chapter, it is that the roots of loving money are deep and strong. They can strangle a faith when they get too deep. So, what is the key to seeking God over money? What does this really entail?

To close this devotion, I want to illustrate the struggle between loving God and loving money. Imagine you are climbing the mountain of financial success. Things are going just as you had hoped, but then you slip and are hanging onto a cliff for dear life. God is there for you, it's just that He is standing at the bottom of the cliff. You know that He is there and can save you from the long fall with ease, but you are still scared and don't want to let go of that cliff. In this situation, letting go and falling into God's arms is clearly the right thing to do, so why don't we do that? Why do we hang on and fight to go higher? Do we fear because we don't see Him, or because we doubt He is there? Regardless of the reason, this scenario makes a great point for all of us to ponder. No matter what financial situation you are in, it is always important to remember that God is there. He knows your needs and will provide for you in accordance with His perfect plan.

Prayer

Dear Lord, please help me to be content and not to focus my eyes on financial success more than You. Amen.

Personal Reflection

Think of a time in your life when you were about to fall from the cliff of financial stability. How did you handle this situation? Did you believe in and embrace God's presence, or did you feel like the fall would lead to disaster?

Day 7

Take Your Pick

24 "No one can serve two masters. Either you will hate the one and love the other, or you will be devoted to the one and despise the other. You cannot serve both God and money.

-Matthew 6:24

THIS DEVOTION IS the final piece of this chapter about money. Over the past few days, my hope is that you have come away from each devotion feeling full and reassured of God's love. Normally I like to end each chapter on a light note, but this one is a little different. We have spent time over the past days reflecting on Scripture and studying the ways that the love of money can pull us away from God. Now it is time for you to answer some questions that the verse above implies. Do you love God or money? Is your life dedicated to serving God, or is it dedicated to making money? These are hard-hitting questions, but we need to be honest about how we answer them. Jesus makes it very clear in the verses above that we can't be dedicated to both. We can't idolize money and focus our eyes on God at the same time. It can't happen. God needs to be #1. So, what do we do? Or maybe the better question is: how do we do that? My hope for today's devotion is that your confidence grows when it comes to answering some of these tough questions. In the moment, you may feel overwhelmed by the thought of completely putting God first. However, I want you to be encouraged in knowing that it can be done.

In this life, it may feel like there are a lot of things that are impossible. For anyone with a deep struggle or addiction, there may seem to be no possible way to overcome it. Let's face it, we know as Christians that we are weak and have a deep need for a Savior. We have sinned and need forgiveness.

As you have probably figured out by now, this is not some cheesy self-help book about how you can be more or how you can be better. We are all sinful. We all fall. This book is not about being perfect, but is about loving God out of thanks for the love He has shown you. In the times when you struggle with things such as idolizing money, don't be discouraged. Rather, be encouraged and know that God knows what is on your heart and is there to help. Remember, there is not one chain in this book you can overcome alone, including this one. Above all things, remember that God is there for you and will help you battle every struggle you face. May God be with you as you strive to put Him first every day of your life.

Prayer

Dear Jesus, thank You for dying on the cross to save me from my sins. I struggle with so many things, including loving money and ask that You guide my heart to seek You alone. In Your name I pray. Amen.

Personal Reflection

As you reflect on this chapter, what was your biggest takeaway? How has talking about topics like money encouraged you in your walk with God?

9

Pride

Day 1

The Dangers of Success

23 Pride brings a person low,
but the lowly in spirit gain honor.

-Proverbs 29:23

WE HAVE STUDIED many chains over the course of this book. Some of them have probably been somewhat distant to you, and others have probably hit you right in the heart from the moment you read the title page. The chain of pride is probably the heaviest in my life. Some of you who know me may be surprised by this, and others may not be surprised at all. Regardless of how well you know or don't know me, I want to be transparent with you about this struggle in my life. Pride is something that burdens the heart and exhibits thoughts, words, and actions that pull God's people away from seeing how He has blessed them. For me, this struggle has made it hard to always acknowledge that God is the giver of all my gifts and abilities. As we study this chain, my hope is that you not only see the importance of being humble, but also see how graciously God has blessed you.

To give you some insight on my struggle with pride, I want to give you a snapshot of my life from the last couple of years. For me, pride has not always been a struggle but is something that came along with the successes that God has blessed me with. For instance, I was an average student during my high school years. My hope was to maintain a B average. In college, I was able to thrive like never before and graduated as an honors student. The abilities I was blessed with were great, but it was, and still is really hard for me to keep my feet on the ground.

Another instance of my struggle with pride can be seen in my writing career. In the beginning, my simple hope was that someone would ready my first book *Walking in Faith*. But as time went on and books kept selling, it became easier and easier to internalize that I was a great writer who deserved honor and praise. There is a reason I am telling you about this struggle, and it is not because I want to show you my accomplishments. I want you to see how pride crept into my life. It didn't just come out of nowhere. A struggle with pride is often something that comes with success. The world will tell us that we deserve to show off when we do something great, but our proverb from today is a great example of why we should do the opposite. Often, God's people are actually brought low or bogged down by success on this earth. This is very sad, but true, and my life is an example of how true this is. Please join me in always trying to remember that humility is the key to gaining Godly honor. If we focus our hearts on Him and always give God the credit for our success, there is no doubt that He will bless us even more than this world claims it can.

Prayer

Dear Lord, please humble my heart and help me to see how graciously You have blessed me. Please guide me to honor You in all that I do. Amen.

Personal Reflection

Think of a gift or ability in your life that causes you to be prideful. In light of our proverb from today, say a prayer and ask God to help you in your efforts to be humble.

Day 2

Know Your Value

³ If anyone thinks they are something when they are not, they deceive themselves.
⁸ Whoever sows to please their flesh, from the flesh will reap destruction; whoever sows to please the Spirit, from the Spirit will reap eternal life.

-Galatians 6:3, 8

HOW MUCH DO you think you are worth? That may sound a little silly to ask, but I would really like you to reflect on this. If you could hang a price tag on yourself, what would it say? Would it say $10,000? $1 million? $1 billion?! Personally, I don't know what my tag would say, but it would be tempting to put a pretty big number on it. If we are all being honest, there is a part of us that sees value within ourselves, which can be a good thing but is not always that way. Today's devotion is all about digging deep to see and understand what we are worth and why we have value.

As you look at the verses above from Galatians, you may be a little disheartened. It can be hard to deal with the reality that we are not great on our own. We all want to believe that we are a big deal and that we make a big difference in the world. Often, we measure our value by comparing the good we do to what others do. In Galatians 6, the apostle Paul is referencing the importance of doing good. However, I want to encourage you to look to these verses as a great reminder of how we have a means of doing good works and why we do them. Pride is a chain that becomes very heavy when the purpose behind our efforts shifts from God to the world. It can be very hard to keep our focus in the right place in a world that is so focused on serving sinful desires. So, how do we redirect our focus? If we are not focused on serving a world that sees value through works, then how will we ever know what we are worth?

When it comes down to what you are worth, what if I told you that you are worth more than money could buy? What if I told you that we are worth blood, sweat, agony, and death? As Christians, we all know the great truth of what Jesus did for us. He did it all! He lived perfectly. He suffered and died on the cross and rose again on Easter Sunday to redeem us from sin. Our value in life will never be established in what we do. Don't get me wrong, doing good works out of love for Christ is very important, but never forget that your works are not the source of your value. They are a way of showing God love. Your value and mine is found in the fact that our perfect Savior paid our way to Heaven. The gift of faith is where our value is found, and my hope is that you never undervalue that. Always remember that your value is not found in what you do. It is found in what Jesus has already done for you.

Prayer

Dear Jesus, thank You for dying on the cross to save me from my sins. I know my value is found in You and ask that You help me to never forget this amazing truth. Amen.

Personal Reflection

What are examples of abilities or possessions that give you value in the eyes of the world? How can you better embrace the source of your true value from this point forward?

Day 3

From Where All Gifts Flow

[16] Don't be deceived, my dear brothers and sisters. [17] Every good and perfect gift is from above, coming down from the Father of the heavenly lights, who does not change like shifting shadows.

-James 1:16-17

WHAT WOULD YOU consider to be your biggest accomplishment? That thing you have done that stands out when you look at your life as a whole? For me, writing *Walking in Faith* (my first book) has been that pinnacle element in my life for years now. Among all of my accomplishments, writing and publishing that book has stood out in my mind as that great accomplishment I am known for more than any other. Now, what if I told you that everything surrounding your accomplishment or mine is a gift? That it's really not about us or what we did, but about what has already been done for us. Today, we are going to dig into Scripture and study the source of everything we have.

There is a part of every Christian that gives thanks for what God has given us, but is there also a little part of us that doesn't want to acknowledge these words from James as true? Personally, there is almost always a battle between my faith and my human flesh about the meaning behind these words. There is a part of me that wants to take full credit for *Walking in Faith*. A part of me that wants to say that the book has my name on it and that it is my work. The world around us wants us to believe we should give ourselves praise and honor for what we do. There are even religions that practice the praising of oneself. Giving God the credit is not a popular move in our world, but is there really any other way to honestly give credit where it is due?

Before pride became a big struggle in my life, I can remember writing *Walking in Faith* and being super thankful that God gave me the gifts and abilities to complete it. If I am digging deep and seeking God's truth with my whole heart, I know that *Walking in Faith* would be nothing if God wouldn't have given me the gifts and talents to write it. The wisdom to write on Scripture is rooted in the gift of the Holy Spirit alone. All of the gifts and abilities that went into that book are from God. It is all from Him, and it all adds up to an amazing set of gifts.

I close out just about every day with a prayer. In that prayer, I ask God to help me with my pride. I know He is the source of every blessing that I have, but my thoughts, words, and actions often fail to reflect what God has given me. Regardless of how pride affects your life, my hope and encouragement is that you will join me in asking God to help us praise and thank Him every day for all the gifts and abilities He has given us.

Prayer

Dear Father in Heaven, thank You for all the gifts and abilities You have graciously showered on me. Please help me to always give You the credit for everything that You use me to accomplish. Amen.

Personal Reflection

I want you to think back to the accomplishment you came up with at the start of this devotion. Now, look at each individual element of this feat and explore all of the gifts God gave you that enabled you to accomplish this.

Day 4

Smart vs. Wise

² When pride comes, then comes disgrace, but with humility comes wisdom.

-Proverbs 11:2

D O YOU CONSIDER yourself to be a smart person? Are you someone who did really well in school or thrives in their career? There are a lot of different views the world takes when it comes to being smart. There are book smart people and street smart people. Some have a photographic memory and others are considered smart because of the time they put into learning a skill. Regardless of how you observe being smart, it is important to see and understand that there is a deeper source of knowledge that is wisdom. Wisdom is something that is divine. It cannot be obtained from human understanding but is a gracious gift that comes from God. In our devotion for today, we are going to dig into another proverb to see the relationship between pride and wisdom.

The proverb above is rather short but is loaded with great information. As we have already learned by now, pride doesn't do us any good. This chain is not something that raises us up as the world may claim but rather breaks us down and actually disgraces us. There is nothing we have done that God hasn't enabled us to do. Humility on the other hand is the inverse of pride that we want to seek. This proverb does a great job of showing a relationship that God's people ought to acknowledge. Humility and wisdom are a packaged deal. They come together like a burger and fries. Godly wisdom cannot be found without humility. One of the greatest temptations I face with pride is thinking that I have the wisdom to figure life out on my own. These words do a great job of reminding me that it can't be done! There is no way that you or I can obtain Godly wisdom without being humbled in the knowledge that everything is a gift from God.

There is a lot of temptation from the world to think that being smart and being wise are the same thing, but don't be deceived. God is the source of wisdom and graciously gives it to those who seek it. Pride may seem like it is the ticket in this world, but never forget that true wisdom can only be found through the gift of the Holy Spirit.

Prayer

Dear Holy Spirit, please guide me to be humble, and grant me wisdom to understand the way I should go. Please help me to resist the temptation to believe that prideful intelligence is superior to Your dwelling within me. Amen,

Personal Reflection

The world has a lot of ideas about what it means to be smart and wise. Based on our devotion from today, reflect on why humility is so important in our lives of faith. What are some sources of temptation in your life that lead you to be prideful when it comes to your own intelligence?

Day 5

Benefits of Humility

³ Do nothing from selfish ambition or conceit, but in humility count others more significant than yourselves. ⁴ Let each of you look not only to his own interests, but also to the interests of others.

-Philippians 2:3-4

I F YOU WERE asked to make a list that put the people in your life in order from the most to least important including yourself, where would you fall on that list? Would you be first, last, or somewhere in the middle? There are a lot of external sources in our life that say we are deserving of many things. That we should have the best and treat ourselves like we are #1. Personally, it is really hard not to put myself at the top, and maybe you can relate. Today's devotion is all about how pride and humility play into our relationships with others, which impacts our relationships with God. There are a lot of mixed signals in this world about how we should view ourselves, and that is why it is really important to get perspective from the only opinion that truly matters.

The verses above from Philippians probably make a lot of sense to most of us. It is known as good and noble to put the interests of others before our own. That being said, I want to take a step back and reveal what happens when humility is not practiced in how we treat others. Selfishness and conceit come from being prideful. Remember, pride in oneself is a singular focus. It does not seek to love others or God. It only zeros in on loving me, myself, and I. These verses from Philippians are a great reminder of how beneficial humility is not only to our personal souls but to those around us. When we lead with a servant's heart, we are not only honoring God but are also being positive representatives of Him in the world around us. Regardless of what you or I have done, we are not that great. We have done nothing compared to what Jesus has done for us. Pride in ourselves shows the world what a sinful person looks like. Humility shows the world the love of Jesus. When you compare the two options, it is pretty clear what we should do. This world needs more Jesus! There is no doubt about it, and we are called through faith to imitate the servanthood that Jesus showed us in His time on Earth. It is far from easy to put others before ourselves, but remember that you are never alone. God has given You His Spirit through faith and has enabled you to do more than you ever could on your own. May God be with you as you strive to live as a humble servant for Him in a prideful world.

Prayer

Dear Jesus, please help me to live as a servant just as You did in Your time on Earth. Thank You for the presence of the Holy Spirit in my life. Please guide me to always put the interests of others before my own. Amen.

Personal Reflection

Evaluate times in your past when you put yourself before others. What are some things you could do in the future to better serve God and your neighbor in how you put the needs of others before your own?

Day 6

Pride in the Lord

²³ This is what the Lord says: "Let not the wise boast of their wisdom or the strong boast of their strength or the rich boast of their riches, ²⁴ but let the one who boasts boast about this: that they have the understanding to know me, that I am the Lord, who exercises kindness, justice and righteousness on earth, for in these I delight," declares the Lord.

-Jeremiah 9:23-24

WHEN IT COMES to pride, we are often tempted to boast of traits we have. For example, there are several traits I have that tempt me to be prideful. God has blessed me with a fit body. He has given me cognitive ability that has enabled me to graduate from college and excel in other ways of life. The point is that God has blessed me with many gifts and talents as I am sure He has done for you. That being considered, what if we were looked straight in the eyes by God and told that all of the things you and I listed are completely meaningless in the grand scheme of things? That all of the skills, gifts, and possessions were as valuable as a pile of dirt. As we dig into our Scripture reading for today, I want you to ask yourself the question: what truly matters?

Upon looking at the words above from Jeremiah, I wouldn't be surprised if you are a little frustrated. Personally, it is hard for me to look at these words and engrave them on my heart. There are times it would be nice (and not to mention a lot easier) just to give a fist pump and celebrate my accomplishments and possessions. There is a part of all of us that wants to take ownership of what we have or what we have done. However, as you dig further into these verses, there is a very central truth that is important to remember when it comes to pride. When it comes down to the things we accomplish or the things we have, they have no value compared to our faith. The question that comes forth from these verses is not *why can't I boast*, but rather is *why would I boast?* Through faith it becomes evident that there is nothing we do that is worth boasting about in the first place. Everything that we have is a gift from God.

To close today, I want to encourage you to take pride in the most important thing in your life. You have faith that enables you to serve this world in a way that only a follower of Jesus can. Always remember we have nothing to boast of alone, but we have every reason to take pride in the faith that is only ours through the gift of the Holy Spirit.

Prayer

Dear Jesus, thank You for dying on the cross to save me from my sins. Please help me to not take any pride in myself or my possessions but to fully give my heart to showing the world how great You are. I am proud to be a Christian and am thankful for the gift of faith I have. Amen.

Personal Reflection

As you go through the rest of your week, think of ways you can take pride in your faith. How can you better love God by serving others and sharing the message of Jesus in the world around you?

Day 7

Praise God!

³ Praise be to the God and Father of our Lord Jesus Christ, who has blessed us in the heavenly realms with every spiritual blessing in Christ.

-Ephesians 1:3

A S WE CLOSE this chapter on the topic of pride, I want to ask you to say a prayer and ask God to suppress all of the self-pride that you have in your heart. If there is anything we have learned in this chapter, it is that pride can definitely have a negative effect on our relationships with God. Today's devotion is all about putting pride aside and thanking God for all of the blessings He has given us.

Now, I would like you to take a couple of minutes and get out something to write with along with piece of paper (you can use the margins of the page if you would like). Write down some of the blessings that God has given you which enable you to serve Him. From the big things like your faith down to something as small as the ability to serve as a greeter at church.

Once you are done, take a look at the list and just ponder it for a second. Take in the fact that God has blessed you with everything you have just written down. I don't know what your reaction is to your blessings, but my hope is that you have feelings of thankfulness and even amazement. Pride is a chain that likes to serve as a blindfold in our lives. Satan wants us to look at our gifts and abilities and think that it is all about us and what we have done. He doesn't want us to look beyond ourselves to see that every spiritual blessing is a gift from God. Now, breaking this chain is not as easy as taking off the blindfold ourselves. We can't do this alone. Only with the help of God can we truly be humbled by all of the blessings He has given us. The central truth of this book is that no struggle is fought alone. Never forget that God is with you and that He wants to help you overcome the chains that burden your life. Our Savior desires to be closer to us and wants us to embrace His presence. My encouragement for you today is to embrace God's love in your life and thank Him for everything He has done for you. When it comes down to it, it's not about what you or I have done. It's about the amazing things that God has enabled us to do.

Prayer

Dear Father in Heaven, thank You for every blessing in my life. I know that everything is a gift from You and ask that You help me to never take that for granted. Help me to honor You with everything that I do. Amen.

Personal Reflection

Go back to your list of blessings from this devotion and circle a few of them. Take a few moments and ponder how God has blessed you with these few blessings alone. Reflect on how God uses you to serve His purpose and to share His love with the world.

10

Doubt

Day 1

True Confidence

11 Now faith is being sure of what we hope for and certain of what we do not see.

-Hebrews 11:1

H OW STRONG IS your faith? This is not really a fair question and is impossible to answer with any sort of metric, but I want you to reflect on it. How strong is your trust in God? How confident are you in His presence? For many Christians, the chain of doubt is not something that is a constant struggle. Rather, many of us doubt the presence of God when things start going downhill. We get weak in times when disaster and disease plague our lives. We don't feel connected to God because we often don't associate His presence with troubling situations that make the heart feel distant. We are not going to spend this chapter talking about how doubting God reveals a weakness in faith. Rather, we are going to explore what faith is and study examples of weak faith to learn from them. The truth is that our God is amazing, and we have every reason to be confident in what He has done for us.

As you look at the verse above, I want to break it down into two parts. The first part of this reading draws a connection between our faith and what we gain because of it. "Now faith is being sure of what we hope for." Notice that faith is not something that is complex. Our faith in God is simply believing in the hope of Heaven that we have because of what Jesus has done for us.

The second piece of this verse is the difficult part for our human minds to come to grips with: "and certain of what we do not see." Our human nature serves as a huge obstacle when it comes to doubt. In general, we like to see things before we buy them. We almost never buy houses, cars, or any possessions without getting at least a glance of what they look like. Faith is different. We don't get assurance that comes through physical sight. We have to trust God and His Word alone with the faith that we have been given. It can be really easy to doubt God's presence being that we can't see Him. That being said, we are going to dig into some Scripture in this chapter that talks about the doubt of people who knew Jesus in His time on earth. They spent time with Jesus in the flesh and still had doubts, so don't be discouraged. There are times when Satan will tempt us with doubt, but never forget about the amazing hope that we have because of what Jesus did for us. We have an amazing faith that is a gracious gift from the Holy Spirit, but it can only get stronger through the help of God. Be encouraged and keep praying for a stronger faith throughout this chapter.

Prayer
Dear God, please strengthen my faith and guide my heart to be confident in Your presence. Amen.

Personal Reflection
Take a moment and think of past situations that caused you to doubt God. Why do you think you doubted Him? Also, how could you better embrace God's presence in the future?

Day 2

Peter

28 "Lord, if it's you," Peter replied, "tell me to come to you on the water." 29 "Come," he said. Then Peter got down out of the boat, walked on the water and came toward Jesus. 30 But when he saw the wind, he was afraid and, beginning to sink, cried out, "Lord, save me!" 31 Immediately Jesus reached out his hand and caught him. "You of little faith," he said, "why did you doubt?"

-Matthew 14:28-31

HOW DO YOU feel about storms? Personally, I live in a place where bad storms are pretty uncommon. But, for some of you who may live in tornado alley or in the Deep South, a storm is something much more significant. Tornados, hurricanes, and other kinds of natural disasters can leave us with feelings of fear, anxiety, and even doubt. As we dig into our devotion today, I don't want you to just think of physical storms, but of spiritual ones as well. Reflect on how you respond to these instant tragedies in your life.

As you look at the words above, you may wonder why in the world Peter doubted Jesus. I mean, come on! He was right there and was the one who gave Peter the ability to walk on water in the first place. Why would he doubt? Well, as crazy as it may seem to us that Peter doubted Jesus when the wind came, is it really that crazy? I understand that Jesus is not physically with us every day, but God is omnipresent. He is always there for us. One of the great realities we know through faith is that we are never alone, so why do we doubt?

My hope at this point in the book is that you have learned many things about yourself, and more importantly, about God. It can be really hard to read about the fact that we all have a sinful nature that is dragging us down. However, my hope is that you are encouraged by the fact that God is always with us. In reality, we have no reason to doubt. This doesn't mean our sinful nature won't lead us to do the same thing Peter did, but we can see through God's grace that our Savior is always there to give us a hand when we fall. His Word is present in our lives to rebuke us when we doubt and strengthen us when we are weak. Doubt is a chain that victimizes many Christians when storms come, but don't be discouraged. My encouragement for you is not to fray when you have doubts but to pray.

Prayer

Dear Jesus, please help me to not doubt You but to keep on praying for strength when storms come into my life. I know I am nothing without You but also know that I can defeat any struggle with Your help. Amen.

Personal Reflection

Think of some storms from your life that have caused you to doubt. Why do you think it is hard for you to trust God is these tough situations?

Day 3

Doubting Thomas

[24] Now Thomas (also known as Didymus), one of the Twelve, was not with the disciples when Jesus came. [25] So the other disciples told him, "We have seen the Lord!" But he said to them, "Unless I see the nail marks in his hands and put my finger where the nails were, and put my hand into his side, I will not believe." [26] A week later his disciples were in the house again, and Thomas was with them. Though the doors were locked, Jesus came and stood among them and said, "Peace be with you!" [27] Then he said to Thomas, "Put your finger here; see my hands. Reach out your hand and put it into my side. Stop doubting and believe." [28] Thomas said to him, "My Lord and my God!" [29] Then Jesus told him, "Because you have seen me, you have believed; blessed are those who have not seen and yet have believed."

-John 20:24-29

D O YOU EVER find yourself looking to God for a sign? Can you identify with the idea of trying to see some sort of indicator that says what you should or should not do? I have done this more than once and can say that the doubt in my heart was not helpful in anyway. Over the course of the last years, I have constantly been looking for signs to answer questions like: *who is the girl I should marry?* or *what career path is God telling me to take?* Fortunately, both of the previous questions have been answered for me, but I want to make a point of saying that they were answered in God's time. There was definitely a part of me that doubted if God would ever make it clear who I should marry or where I should work, but He did. Today's devotion is all about trusting God when we have doubts about the unknown or even what is known.

Jesus' disciple, Thomas, is probably known best for his nickname "Doubting Thomas." After Jesus had risen from the dead, he refused to believe that Jesus was alive unless he saw Him. Again, it may seem crazy to us that people who lived in the time that Jesus was on Earth would doubt Him, but it is really not that crazy. The disciples were sinful people just like we are. They had doubts despite the physical presence of God. The only difference is that we are assured of God's presence through the Word instead of through seeing Jesus directly. We all struggle with doubt at times, but it is important to always hear God out and to trust Him. Jesus told the disciples what would happen before He suffered, died, and rose again, and there was still doubt and hopelessness among the disciples. We can be assured through the Word of God of the same comforting news that the disciples had. When situations arise that cause you to doubt, have faith and be strengthened through digging into your Bible. There is no doubt that God will bless your efforts to trust Him more and doubt less.

Prayer

Dear Jesus, please help me to trust You more and doubt You less. Amen.

Personal Reflection

When situations come that cause you to doubt God, how do you respond? Think of ways (such as reading your Bible) that you can reach out to God in these times.

Day 4

Place Your Trust Wisely

⁵ Trust in the Lord with all your heart and lean not on your own understanding;

-Proverbs 3:5

O VER THE COURSE of human history, there have been many struggles that Christians have faced. Different sins have plagued various cultures with many griefs. As a citizen of this world, you can probably think of some of the sins and struggles that serve as an obstacle for God's people. As a citizen of the United States, I would propose that doubt, which is rooted in human understanding, is the cause of many issues. Many of us have the privilege of living in a time where we have the opportunity to learn and know more than most historical societies could have dreamed of. Human understanding is a big part of our lives, and that often contributes to the chain of doubt that burdens many of us. As we work through our devotion today, I want you to think of biblical teachings that have become social or political issues due to the fact that they can't be understood by the human mind alone.

The proverb above is one that I hold very close to my heart. One of the things I love about biblical proverbs is that they are short but yet full of meaning. The proverb for today is a twofold truth but is extremely powerful. First off, we are given words of encouragement on how the chain of doubt can be crushed. "Trust in the Lord with ALL your heart." All of it! Not half or 99% of your heart. God wants your whole heart. He wants you to trust Him and give Him your everything. However, I know that the second piece of this proverb is extremely hard to do. We like to place our trust and confidence in things that we understand. The human way is to invest yourself in what you can understand. For example, I won't make a financial investment in something if I don't have a clear understanding of what I am doing. That would be considered to be silly based on how the human mind operates, but that is what God wants from us. He wants our whole heart to trust in Him and His Word even when it doesn't make sense. That is faith, and faith challenges our sinful nature, but never forget that trusting in God is not something you have to figure out alone. You can't scrounge up the strength to give God everything by yourself. It takes faith that is strengthened by the love and support of your fellow brothers and sisters in Christ. It takes prayer and time in God's Word to grow. And above all things, the only way to grow is through the gracious gift of strength that God gives us through all of the means I just mentioned. The chain of doubt is strong and rugged in our world, but never forget that God can help you to trust more and doubt less.

Prayer

Dear Lord, please help me to trust in You with my whole heart. I struggle to place my trust in You when my human mind can't understand Your ways. Please give me wisdom so that I can know You and serve You better. Amen.

Personal Reflection

Go back to the social or political issues I asked you to think of in the devotion for today and pick out one of them. Ponder the one you struggle with the most, and identify when and how it causes you to doubt. Say a prayer that asks God to help you put your full trust in Him and His Word.

Day 5

Faithful and Fearless

27 The Lord is my light and my salvation— whom shall I fear?
The Lord is the stronghold of my life— of whom shall I be
afraid? ² When the wicked advance against me to devour me, it
is my enemies and my foes who will stumble and fall. ³ Though
an army besiege me, my heart will not fear; though war break
out against me, even then I will be confident.

-Psalm 27:1-3

A S CHRISTIANS, WE have the amazing privilege of living in the light of knowing we are loved by God every day. This may not be one of the first things that we think about in the morning, but there is assurance found in the peace that we have. That being said, we all know what it feels like to have doubts. We all fall short of trusting God with a complete heart. The truth is that we need His help. As we dig into our Scripture reading for today, my hope is that you are encouraged and uplifted by the amount of trust that David had in God. Often, it may feel as if no one around you has a strong faith. However, I want you to see through the inspired words of King David that there are people out there who have that trust and can be a source of encouragement for you in your life of faith.

It is hard to make an argument that the words above are not extremely powerful. This man had great faith. He had no doubt that God would be with him through every storm of life. Regardless of who tried to oppose, wage war, or even kill David, he was confident because he knew that the Lord was by his side. This is an example of a person with amazingly strong faith, but that doesn't say as much about David as you might think. This man was not bold and confident because of how great he was. He didn't boast in the fact that he was confident on his own behalf because of what he understood. His

154 | Breaking Chains

boldness didn't come from state-of-the-art war tactics that would secure him victory in battle. This man's faith and deep trust was rooted in his connection with God. He knew that God was the giver of all and trusted that the Lord would carry him through the good and bad times. Don't get me wrong, David was a great leader, but he was only as good as God enabled him to be.

To close today, I want to encourage you to seek a lifestyle that is not only faithful to God but is also fearless when it comes to what mankind can do to us. Despite the fact that we may feel vulnerable when doubt strikes, never forget the amazing truth of God's love. He is always by our side, and because of that we never have a reason to fear.

Prayer

Dear God, please build me up and give me a faith like David had. I am seeking a heart that trusts You. Please help me to be confident in Your truths. Amen.

Personal Reflection

Reflect on what you learned about the faith of David today. Take a moment and put yourself in his shoes. How can you be encouraged, and how can you encourage others through sharing this example of unwavering faith?

Day 6

Freedom

8 Therefore, there is now no condemnation for those who are in Christ Jesus, ² because through Christ Jesus the law of the Spirit who gives life has set you free from the law of sin and death. ³ For what the law was powerless to do because it was weakened by the flesh, God did by sending his own Son in the likeness of sinful flesh to be a sin offering. And so he condemned sin in the flesh, ⁴ in order that the righteous requirement of the law might be fully met in us, who do not live according to the flesh but according to the Spirit.

-Romans 8:1-4

I WANT TO KICK off our devotion for today by asking you to think about each of the chains you have read about so far. Now, identify the one chain that causes you more struggle than any of the others. Pinpoint the actions and emotions that come over you when this chain gets heavy. Are you so tied up with this sin that you seemingly can't escape it? Does the burden of knowing how you have hurt God cause you more hurt and sorrow than the last time you gave into this temptation? Do you question how God could love you after committing such a terrible sin? Do you doubt? The reality of sin is far from pleasant. Satan knows our weaknesses and wants us to doubt God's love when we can't seem to get things right. Today's devotion is not about how terrible we are because of sin. It is about seeing that we have a Redeemer who knows our heart and is there to strengthen us when we doubt in our weakness.

Our verses of the day from Romans 8 are ones we all need to remember when Satan tempts us to think that we are doomed by our sin. Verse one does a great job of setting the stage for the message of today. Many times, it can be easy to know and stand by the truth that

Jesus died and rose for our sins. However, it may be fair to say that we too often forget what Jesus really did. He didn't pay part of the price. He didn't come to make it easier for us to work our way into Heaven. He came to pay the full price so that no one who believes will ever be condemned. Regardless of how big or small your struggle with a given sin is, you are not condemned to hell. Jesus did it all so that your faith alone would set you free.

Doubt is something that all of us will probably deal with at some point. Satan uses many tactics to get us to believe that our chains will chain us down for good. However, know that Jesus has broken the chains of death. The chains that try to pull us away from Him may feel strong and ever-present, but never forget that all of those chains will be lifted on the day when you are united with your Savior in Heaven.

Prayer

Dear Jesus, thank You for dying on the cross to save me from my sins. Please guide my heart to always see that You paid the full price and that my chains will not keep me from eternal life with You. In Your name I pray. Amen.

Personal Reflection

Today's reflection is very simple. Read over the verses of the day from Romans and reflect on them. Give thanks for the fact that there is no reason to doubt if you are going to Heaven. Jesus paid the price for you!

Day 7

Limitless

¹³ I can do all this through him who gives me strength.

-Philippians 4:13

T HIS CHAPTER IS full of encouraging Scripture that has the power to lift hearts that are burdened by doubt. However, I think the message for today is the ultimate confidence booster when it comes to dealing with the chains in our lives. In our time on Earth, there always appears to be some sort of limits, especially when it comes to resisting struggles like doubt. There may be feelings that say we did a little better than before, but I don't know if any of us ever get to truly live with undivided confidence. Satan is always there to put a little voice in our heads that reminds us we are not good enough. The devil may tempt us to believe that God doesn't love us. Even though we have confidence in the cross and what Jesus did for us, there is still room for doubt that says we will be burdened or struggle with certain sins until the day we die. In some situations, you may struggle with a sin until your last day on this earth, but my encouragement today is not to lose heart. As you know from past devotions in this chapter, your struggle is not a one-on-one battle.

The verse above from the apostle Paul is perhaps one of the most encouraging verses in the Bible, but I don't want you to get carried away with it. This verse is NOT saying that Christians with strong faith can achieve or accomplish anything they want because God is on their side. Don't take this as a sign that God will give you wings so you can fly to work tomorrow. Rather, be encouraged in the light of what these words really mean. In this section of Philippians, Paul is talking about spiritual gifts. So, when you take this verse in the context of the work, it is not flashy per se, but is spiritually uplifting. When it comes to serving God and resisting evil, there is nothing we can't accomplish because of where our strength is sourced. We are not capable of serving God on our own but have the power to do amazing things because of the strength He provides. Faith is a very powerful element that we may too often take for granted. Despite how weak you may feel at times, always remember that it is not about what you bring to the table but is really about what God has empowered you to do and accomplish.

For some of you, this chapter on doubt may have been really tough. It is hard to come to grips with the fact that our faith wavers from time to time. However, I hope you leave this chapter with confidence in the fact that you are empowered by God to live for Him. The closer you are to Him, the closer you are to the source of power that enables you to serve Him and others.

Prayer

Dear Lord, thank You for empowering me to serve You in a world that needs You so desperately. Please help me to always be confident in the gifts and abilities You have given me. Amen.

Personal Reflection

When it comes to the chains that weigh the heaviest on your heart, how do you address them? Upon looking at the verse from today, reflect on your prayer life and think of little prayers that you could say to ask God for confidence in His presence.

11

Poverty

Day 1

Where It All Began

⁶ When the woman saw that the fruit of the tree was good for food and pleasing to the eye, and also desirable for gaining wisdom, she took some and ate it. She also gave some to her husband, who was with her, and he ate it. ⁷ Then the eyes of both of them were opened, and they realized they were naked; so they sewed fig leaves together and made coverings for themselves.

-Genesis 3:6-7

TODAY KICKS OFF the final chapter of this book. We have studied many chains and have read a lot of Scripture to this point. For the most part, the last 10 chapters have been about your relationship with God. This one, however, is actually about the chains that burden the world around you. The reality of sin is that it spans much wider than your personal being. The entire world is consumed by this epidemic that started in the Garden of Eden. As we dig into this devotion and this chapter as a whole, I want you to reflect on the question: how can I be a bright light in a dark world?

The verses above from Genesis are probably pretty familiar to you. When looking at the amazing grace of God that is found in Jesus, we often look back to why Jesus had to come to Earth in the first place. It wasn't because Earth is such a nice place full of joy and happiness. There was a sad reality that led to a humble birth, a horrible death, and a triumphant resurrection. Sin is the reality of our world. Jesus came to defeat sin so that we would not be bound by it, but that doesn't mean we don't struggle or that sin evaporated. We still have to face the results of sin every day, so how should we respond? What can we do to have a positive impact on a world that is drowned with sin?

When it comes to the condition of the world, the reality is that there is nothing we can do to change it. Sin will be here until Judgment Day. That is what it is, but don't lose sight of the reality that sin shows us. Regardless of who you are or where you live, you are in need of a Savior. The only way out of a world impoverished by sin is through faith in Jesus Christ. You or I don't have the power to give faith, but never forget that God's Spirit lives in you and can use you to do some amazing things. My encouragement for you going forward into the rest of this chapter is to seek the heart of an evangelist. Embrace opportunities in your day-to-day life to share the Gospel of Jesus with others. His message is too amazing to keep to yourself!

Prayer

Dear Holy Spirit, please guide my heart to share the love of Jesus. Sin may run deep in this world, but I know that His love is deeper. In Jesus' name I pray. Amen.

Personal Reflection

Make a list of your closest friends. Then, put a checkmark next to the names of those who don't know Jesus or are struggling in their faith. Reflect on how you can be a witness for Jesus in your friends' lives.

Drowned in Sin

*⁵ The Lord saw how great the wickedness of the human race
had become on the earth, and that every inclination of the
thoughts of the human heart was only evil all the
time. ⁶ The Lord regretted that he had made human beings on
the earth, and his heart was deeply troubled. ⁷ So the Lord said,
"I will wipe from the face of the earth the human race I have
created—and with them the animals, the birds and the
creatures that move along the ground—for I regret that I have
made them." ⁸ But Noah found favor in the eyes of the Lord.*
-Genesis 6:5-8

D O YOU EVER look at the world around you and wonder if things could get any worse? It doesn't seem crazy to ponder that question being that there are events such as terrorist attacks happening fairly often. People are murdering others for no good reason, and there is enough hate to seemingly wrap around the world at least a million times. We live in a place that is engulfed in sin, but is the time we live in truly the worst?

As you look at the verses above from Genesis 6, there is clear evidence of the worst condition that mankind has ever been in. Many of us live in a place where we are connected to a community of Christians who support us. Noah, on the other hand, lived in a world where he and his family were the only Godly people left. The only ones! The world was consumed with evil to the point where there was no community that served God. Just imagine that for a second. The entire world, with the exception of your family, having hearts that were evil all of the time. Think of how depressing that would be and how much strength it would take to follow God when the ENTIRE world did not. Despite the fact that we have access to communities of

Christians all over the world, it may feel like we are the only ones left at times. However, I want you to be encouraged by this message. God saw the heart of Noah and knew that he was being faithful to Him. Just because the rest of the world had lost touch with God didn't mean that He had forgotten about the few who did still love Him. God knows what is on your heart. He knows that you love Him.

When it comes down to feeling outnumbered in a world that is impoverished by sin, always remember that God sees you and knows you believe in Him. We have the privilege of living in a world that is much Godlier than the world Noah lived in. All that being considered, I want to encourage you to share the love of Jesus with a world that needs Him so desperately. Give thanks for the fact that there are other Christians to look to for encouragement, and always remember that God will be with His people every step of the way.

Prayer

Dear Lord, thank You for the blessing of fellow Christians who are present in my life. Please lift my spirits when I am down and encourage me to share Your love with this suffering world. Amen.

Personal Reflection

How do you perceive the world around you? Is it good, bad, or just sinful? How can you better share the Gospel in times when it feels like there is no hope?

Day 3

Faith in Focus

⁵ Those who live according to the flesh have their minds set on what the flesh desires; but those who live in accordance with the Spirit have their minds set on what the Spirit desires. ⁶ The mind governed by the flesh is death, but the mind governed by the Spirit is life and peace. ⁷ The mind governed by the flesh is hostile to God; it does not submit to God's law, nor can it do so. ⁸ Those who are in the realm of the flesh cannot please God.

-Romans 8:5-8

H OW DO YOU respond when faced with adversity that comes from sinful change in our world? For example, abortion has become a widely accepted practice in the United States and around the world. Rather than being looked at as a sin, it is now often looked at as a human right. This kind of thing is very disheartening, and there is seemingly no way to stop it, so what do we do? How do we respond to a world that looks at things in this way? Today's devotion is all about the direction of our hearts. The reality of living in a sinful world is that God's desires will always be opposed, but that doesn't mean that we have to go along with it.

As you look at the verses above, there are two mindsets that are being displayed for us: one that lives by the flesh and one that lives by the Spirit. As a Christian, it may be a no-brainer to say that we are focused on living by the Spirit, but our world has made this concept easier said than done. Another example of something that is very widely accepted in my neck of the woods is excessive alcoholism. The city that neighbors my home town was rated the drunkest city in the country a few years back. It is not uncommon to see people go out and drink until they drop where I live. Sadly, it is just considered to be an openly accepted part of life around here. How do we respond to things like this? How do we guard our hearts and only seek the truth?

Earth is a very scary place at times. It is hard to have peace when there is not only turmoil between God and the world but also between Christian churches. My encouragement for you in every tough situation is to strive to live by the Spirit. Dig into God's Word and see what He says. Seek the truth in all you do, and stand firm when you are opposed by wrongdoers even if they are disguised as followers of God. It may be overwhelming at times to stand firm in the truth, but don't lose heart. God is with you every step of the way and will send His Spirit to guide you. Living in a world that opposes God is tough and may feel lonely, but always remembered that you are empowered to live by the Spirit.

Prayer

Dear Holy Spirit, please guide my heart to always see and share the truth about God and who He is. This world will tempt me in countless ways to believe many different things, but I know I can be confident because You live in me. Amen.

Personal Reflection

Think of a couple of political or social issues that the world tries to clone as a biblical truth. What does Scripture really say about these things, and who could you go to in order to learn more about what the Bible really says?

Day 4

Know Where You Stand

*18 "If the world hates you, keep in mind that it hated me
first. 19 If you belonged to the world, it would love you as its
own. As it is, you do not belong to the world, but I have chosen
you out of the world. That is why the world hates you.*

-John 15:18-19

HAVE YOU EVER wondered what it would have been like to be one of the twelve disciples? What it would have been like to follow Jesus and to learn from Him? Personally, I think it would have been awesome to have that opportunity. There are tons of questions that I would ask Jesus if He was with me on a daily basis. It seems like following Him would have been simple and comfortable. However, the lives of Jesus' disciples were far from easy. In our devotion for today, we are going to get a glimpse of how the world responds to Christians in general. Our sinful nature makes us vulnerable to attacks from the world, which is why it is important to be aware of what may be ahead. Jesus did a great job of summing up what His disciples could expect from the world because of their faith, and I want you to take what Jesus said and reflect on the question: what can I really expect from the world?

I don't think there is any way to look at these verses from John and feel good about them. No one wants to be hated. We want to feel loved and cherished by the world around us. A personal example of this desire for love can be found in my ministry. My hope over the last years and still today is that people would be encouraged and always respond in love to my efforts to share the Gospel through videos or writing. There is no doubt that I have felt loving encouragement from fellow Christians, but there has also been a flip side to those kind remarks. I have read and seen hateful comments about some of my work because it didn't flow with other worldly ideas. This type of persecution is real, and many times it can be much worse than anything I have experienced. It is probably fair to say that people die every day in our world because they call on Jesus as their Savior. So, what do we do? How can we be strong if or when implications as steep as death come knocking at our door?

To close, I want to encourage you with the lives of the disciples. Out of the original 12 who followed Jesus, only one died a natural death (John). All of the others, aside of Judas, were martyred. I'm not writing this to scare you, but to show you how strong a faith in Jesus can truly be. Those disciples knew that they had God by their side in the worst of times and you should too. This world hates Jesus and may hate you because of Him, but take heart. You have the Savior of the world on your side. And, because of that, you will never be truly defeated.

Prayer

Dear Jesus, thank You for giving Your followers a heads-up when it comes to how the world feels about You. It is hard to deal with the fact that the world hates You and me because of You, but help me to always be encouraged and strengthen my faith when I am weak. Amen.

Personal Reflection

How have you suffered persecution because of your faith? What can you do in the future to better embrace God's presence in these tough times?

Day 5

The End

3 But mark this: There will be terrible times in the last days. ² People will be lovers of themselves, lovers of money, boastful, proud, abusive, disobedient to their parents, ungrateful, unholy, ³ without love, unforgiving, slanderous, without self-control, brutal, not lovers of the good, ⁴ treacherous, rash, conceited, lovers of pleasure rather than lovers of God— ⁵ having a form of godliness but denying its power. Have nothing to do with such people.

-2 Timothy 3:1-5

WHEN DO YOU think the world is going to end? This is a question that has been pondered by many and predicted by some. As we all know, every past prediction of the world's end has been wrong. So, when will the world truly end? When will the world as we know it see its last day?

As we look at the verses above from 2 Timothy, there are a lot of adjectives that are presented as signs of what the last days on this earth will look like. Now, I don't know how you feel after you look at these words, but my gut tells me that we may be living in those times right now! As you go through the list above, I would challenge just about anyone to prove that any of the conditions listed above do not exist. Also, we are currently in the time between Jesus' first and last coming, so it's feasible to think that the last day is not far off. For many, thoughts of the end of the world as we know it are scary. That being said, I want to dig deeper today to see why we have every reason to celebrate that Jesus' second coming may be in our lifetime.

To illustrate the end of the world, I want you to think of it as a 5K run. I have participated in a few of these runs and can speak to the process of running a race. As the run goes on, there is fatigue and maybe even frustration that sets in when things are not going as planned. The longer the race goes on, the harder it gets. However, the feelings of fatigue and pain go away when you cross the finish line. There is a feeling of relief and celebration. The last days of the world as we know it will be tiring and painful for God's people. There will be suffering and there will be tears. However, every discomfort of this world will be lifted from all believers in Christ when it is all said and done. Living in a world that is spiritually impoverished will likely only get tougher, but be encouraged by what Jesus has done for you, and be confident in the gift of Heaven that is yours. This life is our time on Earth to love God and to share His love with the world. Let's make the best of it!

Prayer

Dear Jesus, thank You for dying on the cross so that I could inherit the gift of eternal life. I am so blessed by Your presence and ask that You help me to serve You and others no matter how bad things get. In Your name I pray. Amen.

Personal Reflection

Is the end of the world something that scares you? If so, seek out some scripture passages that display the love of Jesus and plant them on your heart. Reflect on them when things get tough and when the world is burdening your heart.

Day 6

Cling to the Vine

⁵ "I am the vine; you are the branches. If you remain in me and I in you, you will bear much fruit; apart from me you can do nothing. ⁶ If you do not remain in me, you are like a branch that is thrown away and withers; such branches are picked up, thrown into the fire and burned.⁷ If you remain in me and my words remain in you, ask whatever you wish, and it will be done for you. ⁸ This is to my Father's glory, that you bear much fruit, showing yourselves to be my disciples.

-John 15:5-8

THINK OF SOME of the ways you make an effort to be an ambassador for Christ. Maybe you serve in your local church or in a Christian day school. Maybe you serve by doing world missions or service projects in your local community. The key is to think of the ways you serve God. Now, what if I told you that everything you have done to serve God could not have been done alone? What if I told you that the goodness and love in your heart that drove you to do those things is not innate but is only possible through a gift found within? For some, this is knowledge that we carry from the Bible. However, regardless of how you feel about your abilities and where they come from, it is not always easy to swallow that we are powerless on our own. As you have probably figured out by now, today's devotion is not about what we do but is about what God empowers us to do in a world that needs Him so badly.

The verses above are some very strong and empowering words from Jesus about what it means to be connected to Him in an impoverished world. Alone we cannot do anything to serve God. Without the vine of Jesus, we are worth nothing more than a dead branch that gets thrown into a fire. Only through our connection to the Vine do we have true value. Only through being connected to Jesus can we serve Him and the world around us with His love.

To close today, I want to visit a corner of my personal life. I have been writing for a couple years now and have published a few books. I am extremely thankful that God has enabled me to serve Him in this way, but Satan has ways of tempting me to think that my books are my work. My pride gets ahead of me and lifts me off the ground from time to time. From one follower of Jesus to another, my encouragement for you is to stay connected to the Vine. It not only keeps you sourced in the truth, but it also keeps you on the ground. Every good work that you or I have ever done has nothing to do with how great we are but is all about how God's Spirit empowers us to do great things. And, in the end, we always need to remember that we only have eternal life through the Vine that is our amazing Savior.

Prayer

Dear Jesus, thank You for being the Vine of my life. Please build me up and enable me to serve You and the world around me. Thank You for the gift of eternal life that is mine through faith in You. Amen.

Personal Reflection

Think of some ways that God has used You to serve Him in the past year. Now, evaluate how or if you have thanked God for the spiritual gifts that allowed you to do that. How can you better thank Jesus for the blessing of being connected to Him in the future?

Day 7

Lead with Love

43 "You have heard that it was said, 'Love your neighbor and hate your enemy.' 44 But I tell you, love your enemies and pray for those who persecute you, 45 that you may be children of your Father in heaven. He causes his sun to rise on the evil and the good, and sends rain on the righteous and the unrighteous.
-Matthew 5:43-45

I WANT TO GET right to it today and start out by asking a pretty deep question. How do you feel about these verses? Really? They are so counterintuitive to how our human minds work. Generally, when there is evil present in our lives, there is not love to follow. How in the world are we supposed to love people who we consider to be our enemies? How are we supposed to show any sort of compassion or kindness to people such as terrorists or murderers? As we dig into the Scripture that we are going to close out this book with, I don't want you to think about what you can't do. I want you to think about what we have discovered in Scripture over the last 11 chapters and ask yourself what you can do through the Spirit of God living in your heart.

The verses above are ones that serve as a great source of humility. Jesus not only reminds us that we are to love our enemies, but He also reminds us that the good and evil all live in the same world. The sun comes up and goes down for you regardless of what you have or have not done. We all live in a world that is impoverished by sin. We all face challenges and all are in need of a Savior. Despite the hurt and pain that has been caused by the most evil people in the world, they are in need of a Savior too. They need Jesus.

To close today, I want to pose the same challenge for you that I gave myself a while back. When you say your prayers tonight, I want you to pray for someone who it would seem ridiculous to pray for. If there is a name of a terrorist group that comes to mind or just an evil person in general, I want you to pray for them. Pray that the Holy Spirit somehow touches their heart. Pray that they may see the errors in their ways and come to know Jesus. Over the course of my life, I have seen way too many Christians treat evildoers with hate. There is more than enough hate in the world. As followers of Jesus, we are empowered through His Spirit to stand up and love those hard-to-love people. We have strength to pray for those who seemingly don't deserve it. As an ambassador for Christ, my final encouragement for you in this book is to make your best effort to love everyone. It will be far from easy, but all things are possible through the strength that only the Spirit of God can provide. May God be with you and empower you by His Spirit to be a bright light in a spiritually impoverished world.

Prayer

Dear God, please help me to love my enemies. I know that I am not greater than even the worst of people because of sin. Guide my heart to live for You in all that I do. Amen.

Personal Reflection

On the space below, make a short list of people or groups that you consider to be your enemies. Ask God for the strength to pray for these people in the weeks and months ahead.

Permissions and Acknowledgements